"Ted, I have known you for nearly 30 ⌐ I am not sure I have ever shared with you how much of a mentor you have been to me. I would probably not be where I am right not if I had not known you, and I want everyone to know what formidable knowledge, wisdom and FUN you bring around you and this book embodies all of that."

Pierre Noel, Chief Information Security and Privacy Officer, Huawei, Shanghai

"Ted, to those about to rock, I salute you ... and always enjoy listening and learning from you. I always pickup new tips and tricks."

Dr. Eric Cole, SANS Fellow, inventor of over 20 patents, author of numerous books, etc. Washington, DC

"Security is a process and people game. The technology is always shifting. This is a book which helps focus on the individuals who are on the front lines of the everyday security battles. For this, it is a timeless book."

John Strand, Owner, Black Hills Information Security, CTO, Offensive Countermeasures, Spearfish, South Dakota

"The Information Security profession has finally matured to the point where there are great white papers, guides, and books for nearly every esoteric technical topic imaginable. This book, though, is the only one that's focused solely on personal development. It explores the ingredients - the methods, tools and techniques - that set top Infosec professionals apart from the crowd. In the same way a cube of ice can open up the flavors and aromas of a fine Irish whiskey, this self-help guide distills the secrets of success down into a wonderfully palatable mix of humor and good advice about how to stand out in a crowd of super-smart, talented people. If you're serious about launching your effectiveness as a practitioner and your career to the next level, RTFM."

Cindy Murphy, President at Gillware Digital
Forensics, Madison, Wisconsin

"Ted provides practical advice to help you become a modern security professional who goes beyond technical skills to advance to the next level. Read this book to learn how to create more value for your organization and ultimately the most value for yourself."

Frank Kim, CISO and Curriculum Lead, SANS
Institute, San Francisco, California

"Attending one of Ted's Infosec Rockstar talks changed my professional trajectory as a digital forensics practitioner. Ted has this amazing ability to help geeks and nerds like us who love science and technology, to become better versions of ourselves by equipping us with strategies to really make a difference beyond just our technical and scientific expertise. Ted's passion for improving cybersecurity in the world starts with his passion for making us the best cybersecurity professionals we can be."

Jason Jordaan, Principal Partner, DFIRLABS, South Africa (and SANS Community Instructor)

"The InfoSec Rockstar book is something that you will want to reread on a regular basis as you contemplate your career in cyber security. It will inform you, inspire you, and cause you to evaluate the trajectory of your career. Every time I revisit the material, I gain new insights to apply to my personal growth as a security professional. In fact, I've recommended it to all of my colleagues and those I mentor."

Kenneth G. Hartman, SAP, Palo Alto, California

"Ted has been responsible for improving the way I approach clients, and tackle projects. His approach is more atypical, but it tends to be a more personal and tailored approach, aiming to benefit the audience, client, etc. as much as possible. By employing this in my day to day activities I noticed that I build much stronger and trusted relationships, both professionally and personally. Ted, keep on moving forward!"

Larry Vandenaweele, Security Consultant, PwC, Brussels, Belgium

Infosec Rockstar

INFOSEC

HOW TO ACCELERATE YOUR CAREER
BECAUSE GEEK WILL ONLY GET YOU SO FAR

TED DEMOPOULOS

NEW YORK

NASHVILLE • MELBOURNE • VANCOUVER

INFOSEC ROCKSTAR

How To Accelerate Your Career Because Geek Will Only Get You So Far

Published in New York, New York, by Morgan James Publishing. Morgan James is a trademark of Morgan James, LLC. www.MorganJamesPublishing.com

The Morgan James Speakers Group can bring authors to your live event. For more information or to book an event visit The Morgan James Speakers Group at www.TheMorganJamesSpeakersGroup.com.

ISBN 9781683504825 paperback
ISBN 9781683504832 eBook
Library of Congress Control Number: 2017902896

Cover Design by:
Chris Treccani
www.3dogdesign.net

Interior Design by:
Chris Treccani
www.3dogdesign.net

In an effort to support local communities, raise awareness and funds, Morgan James Publishing donates a percentage of all book sales for the life of each book to Habitat for Humanity Peninsula and Greater Williamsburg.

Get involved today! Visit
www.MorganJamesBuilds.com

CONTENTS

FOREWORD

M any people grow up admiring, envying, or wanting to become a Rock Star. The fame and money that come along with them are things often desired. My question to you is, why can't you be a Rock Star?

It is amazes me how people put limits upon themselves. I often hear, "I could never become famous or make a big difference in the world," and my response is, "You are absolutely right based on your mental state. Never trying something is guaranteed failure." If you have certainty and give it 100% you can do anything you want—and that is the mentality of a Rock Star. One of my favorite songs is Journey's *Don't Stop Believin'*.[1] Ask yourself every day what one thing is you can do to achieve Rock Star status. If you are not sure, then this book is for you. Ted will take you through the process. The only thing you have to decide is, do you want to sit on the sidelines and complain or kick some ass and do great things?

Rock Star status is often associated with musicians. As a product of the '80s, I think of AC/DC, Motley Crüe, and Bon Jovi. While Rock Stars certainly exist in the music industry, you can be a Rock Star in any industry. In its most basic sense, a Rock Star is someone who has recognized mastery in a given field. There are really two

---

1   Perry, Steve, Neal Schon, and Jonathan Cain. *Don't Stop Believin'*
     Journey. Columbia Records, 1981. Vinyl recording.

key components: 1) being recognized, known, or sought after, and 2) mastery or expertise in your field. This book is about the first.

The fact that you have this amazing book means you want to be an Infosec Rock Star. With geeks, the missing ingredient is the "recognized" component. Most of us have some level of mastery, we just need to work on the non-technical skills. Being a geek implies you have the technical expertise and are regularly increasing it, but the real question is, are you getting the credit and making the money you deserve?

I'm struck by how many brilliant people are not reaching their full potential. One of my favorite quotes is, "If you don't build your dream, someone will hire you to help build theirs."[2] The question you have to ask yourself is, are you building your dreams or building someone else's? If your dreams align with someone else's then good, but more often I see people doing all the work, building someone else's dreams, and making someone else rich.

One of the many reasons I love the Rock Star analogy is it puts the power and the compensation with the talent. When you are a Rock Star, you are the talent and you make most of the money. You do not see a Rock Star flying in economy while their agent flies in a private jet. That is not how it works. The Rock Star is compensated and fully acknowledged for their talent.

Much of corporate society is broken. Often in a corporation the Rock Star does the work, but some (perhaps average) executive who is not directly responsible gets all of the credit and money. How many times have you built a product or delivered a solution to a customer, yet you received a very small percentage of the revenue or credit, and the non-Rock Star executive who did nothing to directly impact the results or revenue received most everything?

2   Gaskins, Tony A. *The dream chaser: if you don't build your dream, someone will hire you to help build theirs.* Hoboken, NJ: Wiley, 2017. Print.

The reason I bring this up is because many bosses and executives do not want Rock Stars. The reason is that they know how amazing you are, but if they tell you, they will have to cede more control and pay you more money, which they do not want to do. To prevent you from becoming too powerful they will tell you that you are replaceable, that anyone can do your job. If you work on an assembly line you are replaceable. If you are generic you are replaceable. If you are a Rock Star, you are leveraging your unique abilities, and we all have them, and you are anything but replaceable.

Do you want to unleash your full potential and be what you were born to be? Stop listening to others or being driven by fear. If you are ready to embrace your full potential, then listen to Ted and unveil your inner Rock Star and anticipate that life will never be the same.

Stop accepting the status quo for your life and your career. To become the true Rock Star you were born to be, you have to continuously push yourself and get out of your comfort zone. Do not be afraid to try new things. If you never fail, you never live. However, fail quickly, learn, do not repeat mistakes, and use all lessons as an opportunity to grow. Let's try new things this year. Change is good, and as true rock stars Mötley Crüe say, "All Bad Things Must End."[3] If you are ready to end building other people's dreams instead of your own, take this book, embrace this book, and live this book. To those of you about to rock, I salute you.

Dr. Eric Cole

---

3   Sixx, Nikki, Mick Mars, James Michael, and Tommy Lee. All Bad Things Must End. Mötley Crüe. Bob Rock, 2015. MP3.

INTRODUCTION

've written this book for two primary audiences: people who have been in security for a relatively short period of time, and Infosec professionals with a solid skillset whose careers have not progressed as far or as fast as they'd like.

My first few years into my career, I concentrated solely on technology and never considered other knowledge or skills as remotely worthy as technical ones. If you are at this stage of your career, you'd best understand that professional skills like reading and writing, simple social awareness and ability, planning, speaking, leadership, influence (you may prefer the term "social engineering"), time management (which really is just getting out of your own way), and several others, can make an enormous difference, propelling you toward Rock Star status much faster. This book can help you improve those skills exponentially.

The second audience is those who have been in security for a while, perhaps five to ten years, and may have done some really cool things in the field, but their careers and their lives have not progressed as far or as fast as they'd like. People who fall into this audience think they haven't been lucky. Trust me, I understand this! This described me not long ago. What I've learned along the way is that we make our own luck. Networking, speaking at conferences, and continually developing your skills betters your chance of greater success coming your way.

Careers aren't natural progressions. The key is leading a career that has more ups than downs with a long-term upward trajectory of success. I've certainly done well in my life and professional career, but I could have done much better earlier.

What qualifies me to write this book? It's not that I fly around the world regularly, speak on Infosec far and wide, and work on very rewarding international projects. It's not that I swill great Champagne (I am a Champagne geek) and visit places like the Pyramids and The Taj Mahal on days off. It's not my more than twenty-five years in the trenches doing work I mostly love and that makes a difference. It's a great life for me—but not for everyone.

What qualifies me is that I have lots of friends I consider true Infosec Rock Stars, both famous and below the radar, who have freely shared what they believe it takes to be a Rock Star. They make an enormous difference in our field and hopefully our world, and are enormously successful.

And with that, I'd like to thank the folks who have helped with the Infosec Rock Star Project and this book. Many more have offered their thoughts but don't want credit, and my apologies to those I've missed in three years of interviews, both formal and informal, which really were discussions with friends.

In other words, I wrote this with a little help from my friends . . . Eric Cole, Ed Skoudis, Bruce Schneier, Brian Krebs, Alan Paller, Pierre Noel, Cindy Murphy, John Pescatore, Eric Conrad, Clement Dupuis, Stephen Northcutt, Chris Crowley, Johannes Ullrich, James Lyne, Justin Searle, Hal Pomeranz, Josh Wright, Kevin Johnson, Jim Curtin, Bryan Brake, The Rock and Roll Guru, Kenneth G Hartman, Stephanie Vanroelen, Monique Hart, Micah Hoffman, Joe Eckhout, Scott Wright, Kevin Fiscus, Thomas F. Hart, Andrew Smith, John

Strand, Steve R. Jones, Doc Blackburn, Amna Almadhoob, Suzy Northcutt, Adrien de Beaupre, Russell Eubanks, Randy Marchany, James R. Slaby, Larry Pesce, Craig Rosewarne, Frank Quinn, Brian Gerdon, Jennifer Barna, Nathanael Kenyon, Jockel Carter, Carlos Cajigas, Keith Croxford, Kai Roer, Susie Wallace, Matthew Pascucci, Gail J. Murray, Paula Panasis, Alexia Pappas, Gregory Peccary Day, Amelia Demopoulos and many others who I've no doubt forgotten to list (sorry!) or who prefer to remain anonymous.

And interestingly, the friends I do consider Infosec Rock Stars generally consider themselves to be moving toward Rock Star. They are, in fact, quite humble, giving, and modest.

One more thing: make sure you go to http://infosecrockstar.com/bonuses/ and get the extra training videos and resources that go along with this book.

1
OWN YOUR TRAJECTORY

* * * * * * *

S o, what do you want to do in life? Where are you going? What do you want to do when you get there? These are of course obvious questions once you think of them. Are there any dreams, goals, wishes, or desires, you have?

When I was younger I thought the answer was found in becoming more technical. What could be more important than technology?

That's as logical as answering, "Where do you want to go on vacation?" with an answer of how you are going to get there. "I want to go on vacation by car," or "I want to go on vacation by airplane." What could be more important than how you get there? While I sincerely hope you enjoy the journey, where you are going is at least as important as how you are planning to get there.

Technology is *not* the answer. It is part of the solution. For geeks like me and perhaps you, it is a major part of the solution.

Geek is essential. Technical skills are critical. These "technical" skills vary enormously depending on your role. They will be much different if you are a freelance iPhone forensicator, in-house penetration tester for a government agency, contract Java developer, Intrusion Detection analyst for a large oil company, or CISO.

"Geek Skills" – our working definition – are the core skills our role or position requires. They are primarily technical, but can include non-technical skills. For example, if you hire technical people, they will certainly include finding and interviewing candidates. If you spend a lot of time teaching and speaking about Infosec, they will include presentation and audience management skills.

Your geek skills are essential, and you do need to continuously work on improving them. We can always get better. In our field where technology, user requirements, risks, and more are constantly changing, continually sharpening your skills is critical.

As an example, in the past year, I have taken a course on advanced enterprise forensics, listened to at least a few dozen webinars and podcasts on various security and technical topics, taken a math-heavy crypto class and have another one coming up, and also done an online course on improv (being in front of an audience does involve improv, so it is a core skill for me). Of course, there are times when I'm overloaded and do far less.

Qualified Security *Professionals*

"Geek will only get you so far" is going to be an understatement soon. We are not off in a silo alone anymore; we are a core part of the enterprise.

Basic business (and social) skills expected of others are expected of us more and more. These include communication, leadership, influence, teamwork, creativity, project management (finishing things we start) and much more.

"Professional" and "Professionalism" are important terms. In the recent past, we could get away with behavior most of the enterprise could not. We were the nerds, the geeks, and most importantly, not integrated into the company. That is not true today.

I'm not saying we need to "comply" or "fit in" (whatever exactly this may mean), but we are now integrated into the business ethos. Individualism is generally accepted for the creative people, and by and large we are and required to be creative in solving problems in our day to day work.

We are at a Time of Unprecedented Opportunity

The opportunities going forward for qualified security professionals are enormous today and that isn't going to change anytime soon. The skills needed are also morphing rapidly.

You'll be learning things both I and many of the Infosec Rock Stars I've interviewed wished we had known years, often decades, ago!

You'll be cutting years off your learning curve and propelling your career forward at a fascinating time in human history!

Information Security is not a "Geek Thing" anymore and never really should have been. It is being discussed in coffee shops, pubs, and cocktail parties these days. There is enormous interest due to highly visible hacks and nation-state activity.

In the last few months, I've had Infosec students from several government agencies, numerous militaries (first, second and third world) as well as many major corporations. Trust me when say that Infosec is being discussed *and* invested in at the highest levels of government and business.

We absolutely have increased interest *and* activity in the Nation-State arena, for organizations of all sizes. Both career criminals and amateur crooks are thriving and many are making millions. Hacktivism, a fairly new concept, is growing.

Systems are becoming constantly more complex, and complexity is the enemy of security: the more complexity, the more potential attack surface. In some ways we are sitting targets. Attackers can come and go, but most of our information systems need to be constantly up and running.

Why the "Rock Star" Moniker?

Apart from the world of Rock and Roll, what is a *Rock Star*? We need some sort of a working definition.

Wiktionary defines *Rock Star* as "A person who is renowned or revered in his or her field of accomplishment."[4] Renowned means widely known, perhaps even a celebrity. This may mean world famous, industry famous, all the way down to widely known in their company or department. Plenty of Rock Stars are locally or niche specifically renown.

Revered means "respected," and unless you are scamming people, you need to be damn good at what you do, as well as effective at getting things done.

While giving my first few *Infosec Rock Star* talks, I asked my first dozen or more audiences what *Rock Star* meant to them. Here is what I got:

Widely known/celebrity – We discussed this above, and of course widely known and celebrity don't necessarily mean people stop you in the streets for signatures all the time. Rock Stars can be locally or niche specifically renown.

Respected – Rock Stars are respected, and respect is earned. It is earned for two primary reasons: for being an expert in your domain (Geek matters, you better be awesome!), and for getting results. For

---

4   "Rockstar." *Rockstar - Wiktionary*. Web. 24 Dec. 2016.

example, I just saw George Thorogood, perhaps best known for his song *Bad to The Bone*, perform last weekend. Musically, he was awesome, *and* he put on a great show. His pure music skills, which are his geek, were fantastic and his showmanship was superb. He delivered!

Confident – Confidence is interesting, and there are entire books on confidence. Simply put, if you are confident, you are more likely to succeed at what you attempt to do.

> *"Whether you think you can, or you think you can't, you're right."*
> – Henry Ford

Rock Stars are confident.

Successful – People mentioned both *successful* and *rich*, and I am grouping them together under *successful*. *Success* means different things to different people. It often includes a component of lots of money as well as more, but quite honestly, many people do not care about lots of money, which may be hard to believe.

Success is something one defines personally.

Passion – Take two people of equal ability trying to succeed in the same area, one passionate about what he or she is doing, and one merely interested. The passionate person will kick ass every time! You cannot compete long term against passion. In the arena of music, there may be musicians that have big hits who are only interested and semi-passionate, but long term, the musicians cranking out hits over decades are incredibly passionate about their music.

It doesn't matter why you are in Infosec. Maybe you started with passion like I did; maybe you needed a job and found one in Infosec; maybe you were attracted to Infosec because of the high pay and opportunities. What matters long term is that you have or develop passion.

Unique – Rock Stars are unique. There is only one Carly Simon, one Mick Jagger, one Bill Gates, one Madonna, one Bruce Schneier, one Steve Jobs. If you are a Rock Star, you are not another cog in the machine.

You are not easily replaced. Could the Rolling Stones replace Mick Jagger? Sure, but they would be a very different Rolling Stones then.

Creative – If a musician only plays songs they wrote decades ago and create nothing new, they are not a Rock Star, they are a Has Been. Just as musical Rock Stars create new music, we need to be creative in Infosec. The world is changing, and especially the world of technology. We are constantly doing things we haven't done before, often that have never been done before, and creativity is obviously required.

Eccentric or "Out There" – Not all Rock Stars or technical people are eccentric, but many are, and we do have that reputation and are given wide latitude to be "different" by others. Creative people are expected to be somewhat "out there."

Technical people are generally creative and respected; sometimes people actually use the word "wizard" to describe us.

Egotistical – Unfortunately, we have the reputation, often at least partially deserved, of being egotistical. Often this manifests itself in thinking that non-technical people are not smart, but in fact there are several types of intelligence and lots of information and many skills that are valuable.

For example, I have lots of hyper-intelligent friends who are not technical, in some cases almost anti-technical, who possess valuable skills I wish I had. As one slightly extreme example, I know a brilliant surgeon who doesn't do email and barely knows how to use his mobile phone.

Can You be a Rock Star?

Well, every Troop of Baboons has exactly one alpha male, The Rolling Stones has one front man (Mick Jagger), a company has one CEO, North Korea has one "The Great Leader" (위대한 수령), etc.

In any one of these groups, however, there can be multiple Rock Stars. Every member of the Rolling Stones is a true Rock Star in his own right. Within any company, there are usually multiple Rock Stars; in fact, it's even slightly possible the CEO is a bozo instead of a Rock Star! And North Korea? No comment.

There are lots of Rock Stars. Can you join their ranks? Maybe! We will explore what it takes. What is true is that anyone can *move* toward Rock Star. Everyone can get better.

"Rock Star status can at least be approached."
–Ted Demopoulos

"Effectiveness can be learned."
–Peter Drucker

As a group, geeks do not tend to know Peter Drucker, but they should. In contrast, anyone in management better know him! He is the author of thirty-nine books, coined the term *knowledge worker*, and was an all-around brilliant dude who's had a lasting and profound effect on how things are done in business. He was an amazingly effective Rock Star! As he says, "effectiveness" can be learned. Rock Stars are effective. Rock Stars are so effective they receive extraordinary results. And yes, I do have a lot of nerve listing one of my quotes before the great Peter Drucker!

The Five Levels to Rock Star

Just like the seven OSI networking layers, where seven isn't magical (they could have picked five, eight, or ten layers and subdivided the functionality differently instead), five levels are not magical either. They are just a convenient framework for discussion.

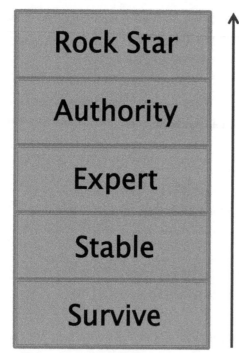

Rock Star	**Specialist:** This is where you Rock!
Authority	This is your area of authority
Expert	This is your area of expertise
Stable	This is what you do
Survive	**Generalist:** You will do anything. You need work!

Notice as you ascend, you go from generalist to specialist. If you are right out of school, you will take most any job. Similarly, if you lost your job and need to pay the mortgage and feed your kids, you will be equally as willing to work almost any job. If you are a Rock Star, like Madonna for example, you are a specialist. You do your own music plus anything else you want – you can do what you want within reason.

Survive – You need a job! If you have a job, it doesn't rock.

Stable – You've got a good job. If you lose it, there may be a lot of effort to find another good one.

Expert – You have developed expertise and Expert status, and have more work choices and flexibility.

Authority – You are a widely regarded and respected expert, distinguished by some combination of innovative ideas, opinions, and intellectual property.

Rock Star: In addition to being an authority, you have more visibility/celebrity, and professional non-geek skills: self-direction, communication, business understanding, leadership, time management, project management, negotiation, results orientation, and lots more.

We will be concentrating on mid-level Stable up to Expert and Authority, focusing on understanding and learning the skills necessary to move toward Rock Star.

If you are at the Survive level, I hope you find this material helpful, although it is not specifically targeted at you. And if you are barely Stable, and this is a continuum, not discreet steps, you've moved in the right direction, and this book is hopefully useful to you as well, although it isn't specifically targeted at you either.

If you are already a Rock Star, awesome! I'm open to feedback!

Infosec Rock Star is firmly targeted for those from mid-level Stable, in which you already have some expert geek skills but may not have expert positioning, on up to Expert and Authority, concentrating on understanding and learning the skills necessary to be a Rock Star.

You do not get to Rock Star overnight; there is work and dedication involved. And just like every sailor can't be the captain, everyone can't be a Rock Star. *However*, and this is incredibly important, we can all move toward Rock Star, be Rock Star level performers, and live a Rock Star life.

What level in the Rock Star progression are you? Regardless of your level, what Rock Star skills do you already have or are developing rapidly?

As an example, I put myself between Expert and Authority. I believe I clearly have Expert status and quite a bit of Authority, but am not yet the Authority I want to be. I'm working on it! I am busy refining my ideas, writing books, generating other intellectual property, and speaking at a wider variety of events than I have at the past.

A couple of Rock Star skills I have are in public speaking and writing, which is interesting as I am a classic introvert and always was a poor writer, at least way back!

What it Takes to Move Toward Rock Star: Geek is *not* Enough

What does it take to be a Rock Star in your field?

Your core technical geek skills are absolutely necessary, but not enough.

Geek is not enough. You can be the biggest and baddest geek in the world—the most amazing iPhone forensics person, for example—but if you smell bad, are unpleasant to be around, refuse to listen to anyone, are unable to ever complete an assignment (never mind on time), your personal life is a mess, and you are a miserable person, your success and influence will be limited.

You need to care about what you are doing, to have at least some passion. Passion can grow, obviously in personal relations as well as professional pursuits. If you do not have or are not building passion, you may be in the wrong field. Of course, some days, weeks, and even longer, our passions, regardless of how intense, may be dormant. That's OK; life happens. But if you have real passion, it will return.

Confidence is also important. It helps a lot, although some amazingly successful people do not have as much confidence as you would expect. You build confidence as you build your skills, and unless you have psychological issues, you will occasionally have some self-doubts. That is normal human nature.

There are plenty of other skills which we'll discuss and ones which we hopefully continually build over a lifetime. Some of these are communication, leadership, time and project management, basic social skills, working well with others, and learning from our failures.

We Exist to Support Our Organization

First of all, we exist professionally to support our organization, and doing well for your organization is doing well for yourself. It doesn't matter if we are hoping to spend a lifetime at our organization, or are actively job shopping, we support our organization while we are there. Of course I mean we "exist" in a professional sense to support our organization. I am not answering deep philosophical questions here!

A Rock Star understands his or her organization. Consultants and contractors likely have several organizations to understand.

Every organization exists for a reason. Why does yours? What does it do? What are its products or services? Simply *to make money* is rarely the ultimate answer.

Every organization has customers. Who are they? What are their concerns? What else do you know or can you find out about them?

"Corporate Culture" is the set of written and unwritten rules on how things are done. If you want to be effective, you need to understand the corporate culture at your place of employment. You learn the corporate culture over time.

Why does your organization exist?

To support your organization, it helps enormously to understand the big picture and know your organization's mission: to know why it exists. An organization's mission is often embodied in a Mission Statement. Organizations spend millions of dollars developing mission statements. Despite that, many companies have atrocious mission statements that ramble on and are even incoherent at times.

"A mission statement defines what an organization is, why it exists, its reason for being."[5]
– Entrepreneur.com

We list several great mission statements below. And even if you have zero input or control into your organization's mission or mission statement, that doesn't make it less important.

▶ **Wounded Warrior Project:** To honor and empower wounded warriors.
▶ **Facebook:** To give people the power to share and make the world more open and connected.
▶ **The Nature Conservancy:** To conserve the lands and waters on which all life depends.

Now it's your turn. What is your organization's mission? Does your organization have a mission statement? Look it up. If there is a mission statement, does it make sense or is it any good in your opinion?

---

5   Staff, Entrepreneur. "Mission Statement." *Entrepreneur*. Web. 20 Dec. 2016.

The Personal Mission Statement

"Outstanding people have one thing in common:
An absolute sense of mission."
– Zig Ziglar

Unlike the mission and mission statement of your organization, you can have a personal mission statement of which you have total control.

"Life is a journey. And your personal mission statement is
your map."
– Anonymous

Stephen R. Covey came up with the idea of having a personal mission statement in *The 7 Habits of Highly Successful People* in 1989. Personal mission statements, which may also be called purpose statements or something similar, are common today, more than a quarter century later.

Yes, I know it sounds touchy-feely, but actually having one written down works. Plenty of research has shown this. It's not like Ouija boards, séances, or palm reading.

When I first wrote a personal mission statement, it was one hundred percent geek. I said, "To play with new and interesting technologies to keep me out of trouble." It was appropriate at the time, but certainly not now.

In writing a personal mission statement, consider what are you trying to do or become as well as what can help you stand out from the crowd. This will need to be regularly revisited and morph over time.

Writing down a personal mission statement or similar and sharing it with others (to help keep you accountable) has been shown to lead to more success.

"I went through this in my own life. At one point I realized I was destined to be a large fish in a small pond, a leading authority in intrusion detection, and network monitoring when there were only about 2,000 analysts that had that as a full time job on the planet. If I wanted to continue to grow, I needed to avoid being typecast for life as an IDS expert but, rather, as a general security expert. We see Tom Peters is right, our personal mission statement changes, we need to find the time to determine what it is, write it down, live it by checking on our progress weekly, and then review it to see if it is still accurate. If you are too busy to create, live, and review your personal mission statement, you are too busy to develop a personal brand, and that is a sad thought."[6]

Personal Mission Statement Examples

▸ Oprah Winfrey: "To be a teacher. And to be known for inspiring my students to be more than they thought they could be."

▸ Richard Branson: "To have fun in (my) journey through life and learn from (my) mistakes."

▸ Sanjeev Saxena, POC Medica: "To develop next generation diagnostics to provide a better life."

Great personal mission statements can be all over the place; very different from each other. They are, after all, "personal."

---

6   Northcutt, Stephen, and Ted Demopoulos. "Living Life on Purpose - Personal Branding." The SANS Institute, Web. 24 Dec. 2016.

I like Oprah's as it is succinct and focused. I like Branson's because it inspires hope and implies that life is fun, at least to me. I like Saxena's due to its laser focus.

Below is a very different one I found on the Internet that I also like quite a bit.

▶ Ronnie Max Oldham: "To find happiness, fulfillment, and value in living, I will seek out and experience all of the pleasures and joys that life has to offer. My core values are not limitations restraining me on this hedonistic quest for fun. Rather, they provide a framework for identifying, pursuing, and achieving those pleasures that last the longest and are the most satisfying. The greatest joy of all is being worthy of the respect and admiration of family, friends, and business associates."

Simon Sinek, Another Viewpoint: "Start with Why"

Your *Why* is similar to a personal mission statement. It might be the same, it might be somewhat different, but they are extremely related at a minimum. We could have a lengthy philosophical conversation on this topic but we won't (at least not now!).

Simon Sinek gave a motivational TED talk called *Start with Why*, which can be found on YouTube. He has also written a book called *Start with Why: How Great Leaders Inspire Everyone to Take Action*. It's great work, and his talk is a great place to get started.

What: Everyone (and every company) can tell you what they do. That is easy.

How: How they do it is tougher, but many can tell you how or at least some of how. For example, I can tell you much, but not all, of what I do to connect with and engage audiences when I'm speaking.

Why: Why is harder. It comes from a deeper and more primitive part of the brain, a part of the brain that doesn't understand language.

It is the *Why* that is most important with connecting with others at a (literally) deeper (brain) level.

Why is not to make money; that is a side effect or result, albeit an important one.

Why is your purpose, your beliefs, your cause.

Ever notice Rock Stars connect with others at a deep level? Take Apple for example, a Rock Star of a company. People (literally) connect with Apple at a very basic level, one that cannot easily or entirely accurately be described with words.

We could say Apple is just a computer company like many others. Why, then, is Apple more creative than all their competitors (probably combined)? It's their *Why*. If verbalized (which is hard), it would be similar to "We believe in challenging the status quo in everything we do. We accept nothing as set in stone. We believe in thinking differently."

Everything flows from their *Why*.

Here is mine: "Learn, Teach, Inspire." We could argue about whether this is a personal mission statement or my *Why*, but it doesn't matter.

I love to learn new things. That is certainly in part why I like Infosec. Things keep changing and there is always a lot to learn. I am happiest when I learn new things. When I learn new things, I love to share the knowledge. I love teaching, and as many of you know I both give lots of talks and teach longer courses on various security topics. There is also lots of knowledge transfer in my consulting gigs.

I don't always inspire others or myself of course, but the new things I'm learning and spreading the knowledge of had better be pretty cool, stuff that can potentially inspire. I find Infosec to be an amazing field with plenty to be inspired by.

Notice that this statement helps guide my decision making.

"Hey Ted, wanna do this <new cool security thing>" – Oh yeah!

"Hey Ted, we can make lots of money polishing ball bearings!" – I like money a lot, trust me, but naaaaah!

Action Step: Future Orientation

Watch Simon Sinek's TED Talk, Start with Why. Google it; it's on YouTube as well as other places.

Write a preliminary Why or personal mission statement. Either is fine.

We will use this to guide our high-level decision making and use the term "Future Orientation."

Do this quickly, within five to ten minutes. Consider it an imperfect draft that you will revisit, make better, and evolve over time. Get something written down, no matter how imperfect. It's just your first attempt.

Of course, some other type of "Future Orientation," like a vision statement, which we'll describe loosely as what you want to become when you grow up, is also fine. Just get something written down.

Serve Your Customers, but Who are They?

We all have customers. We may or may not use the word *customers*, but we have them, whether we work for a government, a non-profit organization, a for-profit company, do sales, internal IT support, external pen testing, or work for ourselves. It doesn't matter; we have customers.

As Bob Dylan said, "You're gonna have to serve somebody," and serving your customers is a major part of supporting your organization. Remember that supporting your organization *is* supporting yourself, so supporting your customers is also supporting yourself.

Customers can be external or internal. We might be selling them some physical widget, a service, providing internal support, or even providing them something they do not really want, like security or audit services. Who your customers are is not always one hundred percent obvious.

An upset or angry customer will tell many others, possibly thousands. Think social media, email, word of mouth, or any other method. A happy customer may or may not tell anyone, but will be easier to work with and serve in the future.

If we get a reputation of being difficult or unpleasant to deal with, our customers will do their best to avoid us as much as possible, and that is clearly not good.

A classic example is *United Breaks Guitars*, a protest song by musician Dave Carroll. In 2008 his $3,500 guitar was severely damaged by United Airlines, and to say his nine-month fruitless negotiations with the airline were frustrating is an understatement. According to Carroll, the initial employees he contacted showed "complete indifference."

The video had more than 150,000 views within twenty-four hours, five million in five weeks, and has had more than fifteen million now. It was a public relations nightmare for United. The very late compensation offer of $3000 failed to undo the damage to United's brand. The *Economist* reports the short term costs to United may have been $180 million.

I've flown the equivalent to the moon and back twice on United, and unfortunately I'm not surprised. I can report that they have gotten better, and may be the only US airline that is actively trying harder to improve, as one of my friends claims. That, however, doesn't undo the damage of the videos that keep racking up the views.

You may think something similar couldn't happen to you? Think again. On a massive development project, I was one of two dedicated security personnel. The two of us were both experienced and knowledgeable, and had similar skills. I had the reputation of being easy to work with and my co-worker had the reputation of sometimes being extremely difficult. I finished the project and happily moved on. He was fired mid-project.

Here are a few things to think about. There are no correct answers.

- ☐ Do you consider your boss a customer? Your boss is a customer of sorts.
- ☐ How about people you provide value to who you may not even know exist? As you move toward Rock Star, this group increases in size. These may be people that read your tweets, buy your albums, listen to your talks, watch you on YouTube, read articles you've written online and more.
- ☐ How about your co-workers? Some may obviously be customers, but what about the others?
- ☐ How about friends you work with? Are they your customers? They might be.

Example: Who Are Your Customers?

Let's look at a concrete example, Demopoulos Associates, which is basically me, a one-man Infosec consulting and training company.

I have some obvious customers, ones who directly or indirectly pay me money. These are direct-consulting clients, The SANS Institute, who I do a lot of training and curriculum development for, along with people who take my Infosec Rock Star classes and other classes.

I also have some non-obvious customers, including people who read what I write online, people who attend (free) Webinars and talks I give, people who watch my videos, and people who read my books.

Some of these non-obvious customers do indirectly pay me when they buy my books from book stores, or through the advertising on my Websites. And some eventually become clients who also pay directly.

Passion

The most successful and most influential people have passion. Passion will give you energy and a sense of purpose.

Maybe it's passion for your day-to-day geek skills job; maybe it's passion for your company; maybe it's passion for the people you work for; maybe it's passion for something higher level, some big-picture mission.

Someone may not see themselves as a passionate person but that doesn't mean it is not there. Most people are passionate about something. It may be their children, or sports, or a hobby, or coaching, or volunteering. Many say you can harness passion and focus it in a different direction. That is definitely true for lots of people. It doesn't matter why you got into Infosec. Maybe you started with passion like I did; maybe you were just looking for a job or a growing field to work in.

Security is not About Geek/Technology

We need to recognize that security is *not* about technology.

Fundamental security concepts like Defense in Depth, Least Privilege, Separation of Duties, Rotation of Duties, Confidentiality, Integrity, Authentication, and Authorization, just to mention a few, have existed forever.

Even many things in security we may consider fundamentally technology-based and new are not. Biometrics have existed forever; think personal recognition by a guard. The Ancient Egyptians used cryptography (Hieroglyphics) as did Caesar (the Caesar Cipher), and the Ancient Greeks used steganography (e.g. Herodotus in 440 BC).

Security at its most basic level is risk management. We reduce risk to an acceptable level by implementing controls, which can be physical, administrative, or technical.

What is different today is that many, and for some organizations most, of our assets are not physical. Many are digital and stored on our information systems.

Specifically, because of this, many of our controls are implemented with technology, but security is not fundamentally about technology. This is so easy to forget in the modern world.

Confidence is a Rock Star Quality

"Believe you can and you're halfway there."
– Theodore Roosevelt

Confidence is a Rock Star quality. Don't get me wrong; we all have self-doubt at times. I've been with literal (music industry) Rock Stars who lacked confidence at times.

Being good will help make you confident. A series of successes (punctuated by failures; as always, failures are normal) builds confidence.

Aim to build confidence *without* arrogance! Technical people are often accused of arrogance. I certainly have been guilty of this before. Just because someone is not technical doesn't mean they are not smart. Just because you know something an expert doesn't know, doesn't make them less of an expert. Just because you may be the only person who knows how to do a certain thing at work doesn't make you better than others.

One type of exercise many experts at building self-confidence suggest is to list your strengths. For example, list:

- three physical strengths
- three mental/intellectual strengths
- three emotional strengths
- three social strengths
- three family relationships you are proud of
- three ways you're competent around the house
- three positive talents you have
- three specific things people have loved about you
- three kindest actions you've taken (first three things that come to mind)
- three of the most inspiring goals you have (just three big ones)

Let's Talk Geek Now

Geek will only get you so far, but Geek is required. For math and logic nerds, Geek is necessary but not sufficient for Rock Star status. If you are not damn good and getting better, concentrate on building your core Geek skills.

That said, although people in many fields think they are far better than they are, I find technical people, and especially Infosec people, tend to underestimate their skills. I have worked with scores of Infosec people, including in leadership and management, who thought they were "not technical" but in reality were. Perhaps it's because there is so much to learn, perhaps because we all work with "ultra-geeks," or maybe it's something entirely unrelated.

In any case, Geek is essential, but what constitutes geek skills will vary depending on your role and position. I often include non-traditional core geek skills in my definition, depending on the role. For example, when hiring pen testers, I'd include the ability to find, interview, and hire pen testers as a geek skill for you, and since I spend many weeks a year presenting technical topics I'd include presenting technical topics as a geek skill for me.

Clearly we need a strong, broad base of technical knowledge. Take a look at the SANS GSEC outline or CISSP CBK to see the diversity of skills that are great to have a basic knowledge of.

We also need to specialize, and we are more and more becoming a group of specialists, just like medical doctors and others have become.

A musician cannot play everything beautifully: the drums, sitar, guitar, ukulele, piano, flute, violin, rock, blues, jazz, classical, flamenco, disco, etc. Similarly, you need to specialize. You probably can't be a great IDS analyst, mobile forensics guru, brilliant pen tester, and router security person.

Specializing does not necessary limit you to just your specialty. Hey, Jerry Garcia once played bass on April Fool's Day. And a Fortune 500 company once asked me for corporate restructuring advice when I had been hired as a relatively lowly Infosec guy.

We naturally trust specialists more than generalists. Who is smarter and more trustworthy, a medical doctor in general practice or a brain surgeon? I suppose it depends on exactly what you need and the specific doctor, but we tend to mentally position specialists more highly.

Basics: Communicating with Others

Communicating with people similar to us is relatively easy. Communicating with people unlike us is more difficult. Personally,

I communicate with most Infosec people much more easily and naturally than with sales people, financial folks, and goat herders. In a small company, people are connected and communication is relatively easy, even among people with very different backgrounds. As organizations grow, different subcultures develop each with their own idioms and terms. The same word or phrase may have quite different meanings within different parts of an organization.

Research in the fields of Organizational Development and Organization Psychology strongly suggests that as an organization reaches about 500 in size, this fragmentation occurs. Even similar groups develop different subcultures, each with their own idioms and terms.

Think about an organization with thousands of technical people: different groups of even technical people will have some difficulty communicating with each other. Most of you have experienced this!

Trust

Trust is essential, especially in security. It helps enormously in communications, teamwork, leadership, and much more. Also, although people will forgive you for making mistakes, they will not for ethical lapses and issues of trust. Make it a point to find out why people do or do not trust you. Send a brief email to those you work with and who know you best.

It's Never Straight Up

"Success is not final; failure is not fatal; it is the courage to continue that counts."
-Sir Winston Churchill

No career, no life, not much of anything is straight up. Ups and downs, sometimes massive, are normal.

I assure you I didn't feel like a Rock Star when I was recently jetlagged in the Middle East trying to teach a six-day boot camp in five days at a large oil company that preferred the course in a more traditional format.

After my son was born, I took many months off due to his medical issues (he is fine now and a normal, difficult teenager) and restarting my career later was absolutely a challenge.

There are plenty of other "downs" I could mention, both professional and personally, but as Rock Star Joe Walsh says, "Life's been good to me so far."

Learn to embrace failure. The most successful person has plenty of failure and often sees it as a positive learning experience, at least in retrospect. Mindset matters, sometimes a lot.

Winston Churchill said, "Attitude is a little thing that makes a big difference." I couldn't agree more!

Rock Star: It's Simple but not Easy

I'm not writing and teaching to help you stay on your same path. Becoming an Infosec Rock Star is more work than turning on the TV and popping a beer. Moving toward Rock Star status is simple, although it's not necessarily easy.

There is work involved. You will need to get out of your comfort zone at times to become a Rock Star, just like a lobster. A lobster? Well, lobsters need to regularly shed their hard shells in order to grow. When they shed their hard, protective shell for a new, initially ultra-soft one, they are truly out of their comfort zones and vulnerable. Although lobsters are usually extremely vulnerable because of this so called "molting," they can grow over eighty pounds and they live a very long time.

Just like a lobster, in order to grow, to move toward Rock Star status, you are going to need get out of your comfort zone sometimes. You're going to need to look at some new ideas and try new things that may not be in your current comfort zone. We are just looking at pushing the edges of our comfort zones, not leaping entirely out of them. For example, if you have a fear of public speaking, you certainly do not need to start by speaking to an audience of ten thousand people. Presenting to a small group of your peers, perhaps your department, is a more reasonable initial step. Just like I am afraid of heights, I won't be skydiving or bungee jumping any time soon. Climbing a footstool is a more reasonable first step.

In the next sections you will see that everything we discuss is pretty simple. Doing it is not necessarily easy, but it's all simple.

Success

A Rock Star by definition is successful. If you are not successful, you are no Rock Star.

But what is success? It is clear that the definition of success varies by individual, and successful for me might be miserable for you, and vice versa. The definition of success varies by individual.

Maybe you go to work every day, work on cool projects, and then come home to your wife and kids or girlfriend or boyfriend or pet goats, and take a couple of mind-blowing vacations every year. Sounds great, but that would bore me. No offense. Success is personal.

It is also clear that success is a moving target.

What I consider successful today and what makes me happy (and I'm pretty dang happy and successful right now) just won't cut it in the future. Life is supposed to evolve, we are supposed to grow, and success and happiness are moving targets. This is normal.

Success is more than just money. Although success has a money component to most of us, that is not all. Some of us have financial goals, but you can be making boatloads of money and be miserable, and that is not success. Believe me; I tried it once.

And I'm sure you can be poor and happy (I haven't tried this though), but rich, or at least well off or not hungry, and happy is way better.

For some of us, success involves freedom from routine. Freedom is an enormous part of success to me, which may help explain why I haven't had a full-time job since 1990.

So, what makes you happy?

Do you have any short, medium, or long term goals? Or maybe you are just coasting on past successes for a while. We all coast at times.

Just remember, once you reach your goals, your feeling of success may naturally be temporary. Success is a moving target. Or as my friend Rufus says, "There is always a bigger boat."

Success: My quick personal thoughts

- ☐ Continue doing what I'm doing
- ☐ Spend more time with my kids
- ☐ Get and stay in better shape
- ☐ Sit in business class or better on most long flights
- ☐ Make money irrelevant again
- ☐ Provide a lot of value to my communities

I scrawled this down in less than five minutes a few months back and have made progress on most of the items listed. You also need your definition of success.

Some of my ideas of success may seem silly, some may seem admirable. It doesn't matter; success is personal. We cannot judge other's definitions of success, as long as they are moral.

Action Step: Write down a quick definition of success.

It doesn't need to be all encompassing. It can include specific goals or not. Just get something down and don't stress over it. You can change/modify/update it later.

2
OWN YOUR TIME

● ● ● ● ● ● ●

Hopefully it is obvious that Rock Star is not nine to five. Life is not nine to five.

As you move toward Rock Star status there will be more demands on your time, yet you still will have exactly twenty-four hours per day. OK, time geeks, I will admit that "leap seconds" exist, but they are not significant in this context. Given the limited amount of time you need to efficiently use it.

This includes doing the right things, not doing some things which perhaps you used to do, and doing what you do efficiently.

Down-time is important too. No one is telling you to be a workaholic, although there *will* be time crunches and missed sleep occasionally. You'll also need time to rest and recover, and time to do something fun, although being a Rock Star or working toward Rock Star status *is* fun.

I often get some of my best ideas during down-time as do many others. For example, some people have brilliant ideas while "wasting" time singing during unusually long showers. I sometimes stop during bike rides to jot down ideas on my phone.

You are Never Going to get Caught Up

Getting "caught up" is a quaint notion, but it is not going to happen.

It's not like our work is all physical today and we can see it and once we finish what we see (like harvesting a field of crops, or packing a roomful of boxes, or whatever), we are done. There will always be more than you can possibly do.

It would be great to be more productive. We will discuss being more productive soon. However, that alone will not get you caught up.

There is never enough time to do everything you want or think you should do. Conversely, there is exactly enough time for what you do get done.

For example, I have piles of books, PDFs, articles, and more I would love to read, but I'm never going to read them all. There are emails I would like to answer but I'm never going to answer them all. At any time, I have multiple projects going and some could use more of my time. I have some incredibly cool projects I'd love to start and hopefully finish, but realistically I won't. There are people I should reach out to, but I'll never have enough time to reach out to them all.

And of course there are non-work related things too. In my case:

- It would be nice if I could exercise more consistently.
- I want to go hiking in New Zealand again.
- I love the idea of tango lessons in Argentina.
- I would like to fish more next summer.

- I want to travel more and be home more often (hmmm, slight conflict here?).

Future Orientation

"Long-term thinking improves short-term decision making"
- Brian Tracy

Long-term thinking absolutely improves short-term decision making. It doesn't matter what form this long-term thinking takes, whether it is through defining a personal mission statement, long-term goals, your *Why*, a vision statement, etc. (many of these we discussed in the previous chapter).

"If you don't know where you are going, you'll end up someplace else."
- Yogi Berra

Remember the Action Step in the previous chapter where we wrote something down and referred to it as our Future Orientation? It may have been a personal mission statement or *Why*.

This long-term thinking or Future Orientation can determine, or at least greatly influence, current actions. It helps you know what to say yes to, the order you do your yeses in, and what to say no to as well. If it fits in with your future thinking, it's a probable yes. If it doesn't, it's a probable no.

Here are a few questions for you:

☐ How good are you at future thinking?
☐ How good are you at finishing what you start?
☐ How are your time management skills?

☐ Have you improved over the past few years?

Long-Term Thinking: Strategy

Since we can never be caught up, it is important we distinguish long-term thinking, meaning high-level planning and activities, from low-level planning and activities. This helps prevent us from being lost in the weeds, or letting superfluous things detract from other more important or prominent things.

I'm going to grossly simplify something here, leaving out many nuances, but basically we can consider long-term thinking as strategy: what you want in the long-term. We can consider short-term thinking, and the actions it produces, as tactics. We could discuss strategy versus tactics versus vision versus who-knows-what-else for an entire book, and although perhaps interesting, these nuances are not important here.

If we have no long-term plans, no strategy, then it doesn't matter much what we do, as the paraphrase from the Cheshire Cat in *Alice in Wonderland* states: "If you don't know where you are going, any road will get you there."[7]

Of course we do have some idea where we want to go: we have our Future Orientation from the previous chapter to help guide us, as well as our personal definition of success.

Flexibility is always essential. It's not like we have a crystal ball and can see the future. The world, our plans, our thoughts, opportunities, and more may change as we move forward.

Sometimes just stopping and asking (often yourself) "Is this strategic or tactical?" or if you prefer, "high-level or low-level?" or perhaps "in line with our Future Orientation?" can help to clarify

---

7   Lewis Carroll. *Alice's Adventures in Wonderland*. London: Macmillan and Co., 1865. Print.

things a lot. This is assuming we are going somewhere and are not just drifting aimlessly through life.

> *"Strategy without tactics is the slowest route to victory.*
> *Tactics without strategy is the noise before defeat."*
> —Sun Tzu

We will use the terms *Future Orientation, strategy*, and *strategic*. For us, Future Orientation, strategy and strategic simply means high-level. There can be multiple strategic levels; they are all high-level.

Strategy can be a confusing term as it can be defined in rather different ways, including a specific plan, as in the terms strategic plan and strategic planning, it can be a position, or even a perspective.

What everyone agrees about on strategy is that it is high-level and long-term.

Examples:

- ☐ Strategy as a Plan: Yes, I had a specific plan for offering my first Infosec Rock Star Workshop. Some of you may have seen the actual picture of my whiteboard outlining it.
- ☐ Strategy as a Position: This could be, "Our strategy is to offer the best Infosec Rock Star training possible at a fair price."
- ☐ Strategy as a Perspective: "Non-technical skills are now extremely important and will continue to massively grow in importance for security professionals," with perhaps an implicit, "and we are planning the future of our business heavily on this."

Our Future Orientation and also our own definition of success must be in concordance with our strategy, however we may specifically define it. They serve to guide our strategy, our long-term thinking.

Smaller Things: Lower Level "Stuff"

Yes, Future Orientation – the big picture, is critical.

But you don't *do* a big picture, you don't *do* the future, you don't *do* strategy. Instead you do lower-level things.

We'll group lower-level items into two rough categories:

☐ Those that directly relate to the big picture. We will use the term *tactics* for these.

☐ Others are simple things that simply need to be done that do not directly relate to the big picture.

The big picture doesn't change often. Our Future Orientation is not static, yet it evolves relatively slowly. The tactics used to implement it can change far more frequently.

The other things that simply need to be done are not tactical, but they need to be done, and may be urgent.

Some examples from my past few weeks are: get second US passport so I can send one to the Indian embassy while I use one to go to Europe, apply for business visa for India, deal with financial aid paperwork for my daughter, and reschedule medical appointments because of my somewhat last minute European trip. None of these were strategic, but were simply things I needed to do with an annoying level of urgency.

Top Down *and* Bottom Up Thinking

Basing things primarily or solely on long-term thinking is known as *Top Down*.

Figure out the top, whether you use approaches and terms like personal or corporate mission statements, your *Why*, long-terms goals, vision statements, or something else. We are simply going to use the term *Future Orientation*. From Future Orientation we get our critical objectives, then tactics to implement them, then the actual granular details of things to do.

This is logical and works to a degree, but we often lose our sense of Future Orientation in our day-to-day lives. It's hard to maintain your thoughts of the future when you have near daily overload.

Bottom Up thinking concentrates on getting control of what needs to be done on a short-term basis, such as today or now. This absolutely includes things resulting from our future thinking as well as other critical things that need to be done and often pop up rather unexpectedly.

Clearing the decks of these smaller tasks not only helps us move toward the future (some of those smaller tasks will be directly related), but also helps clear the mind and can allow us to be more creative and concentrate on the future. If you are buried in details, you don't tend to be creative or think about the future.

Success Leaves Clues

"Long ago, I realized that success leaves clues, and that people who produce outstanding results do specific things to create those results. I believed that if I precisely duplicated the actions of others, I could reproduce the same quality of results that they had."
– Tony Robbins

Since everything takes time, and time is our scarcest resource, it makes sense to look at what the most successful people are doing and, equally importantly, what the most successful people are not doing. This may or may not be obvious initially. Also, the rules may be different for you. If you're a junior employee you generally will have far less flexibility than if you are a senior employee, perhaps a founder or partial owner.

Consider both what people in your industry are doing as well as people in your company, or your clients if you are a consultant. Think big picture as well as lower level detail.

So what are the major jobs/roles you have had and what were your most successful colleagues doing? It can be very illuminating to analyze both your past and current positions. As an example, let's look at a few of mine. Note the time overlap, as I'm a consultant.

▶ The Open Software Foundation (OSF), 1991-1999

OSF was my first consulting client and a massive client I worked with for many years. Many people there, including the guards, thought I was an employee. The most successful people, both consultants and employees, were passionate about developing and learning new technologies quickly and were politically savvy. All organizations are political organizations to some extent, and as a not-for-profit organization founded by competing computer vendors, of course politics mattered.

I learned new technologies aggressively and had a blast. I was very successful. I would have been more successful long term if I had more political acumen, although I have zero regrets here.

▶ Digital Equipment Corporation (DEC)/Compaq, 1991-2001

DEC was my second largest consulting client. At DEC (which was bought by Compaq and eventually HP) I did extremely well. The most successful people in my role were developing and delivering innovative courses and other material, as well as spreading horizontally in the organization.

I wrote and delivered innovative and unique material very effectively and had a great time. I could have spread throughout the organization better, worked for more groups, like many other consultants did, however.

▶ Cerint Technology Group, 2000-2002

Cerint is my textbook failure of a startup and no one was successful. I was not one of the four founders who were all fraternity brothers from the same college, so I simply wasn't listened to despite being the CTO. I also should have had a written instead of a verbal contract.

I learned a lot at Cerint, but quite bluntly I should have seen the obvious warning signs and fled before it blew up. My analysis: I was a bozo.

▶ The SANS Institute, 2004-ongoing

At SANS, I will not say much due to the open-ended nature of our relationship, however they've been paying me since 2004 so you can I assume I'm happy.

I'll also say the most successful instructors are the ones who develop and deliver new innovative courses, generally within one specific niche, who remained focused, and who are politically astute. Remember that every organization is a political organization! I have not been as focused as I could be and generally have developed less valuable intellectual property for SANS than many, in large part because I have other clients and professional interests, and that's all good.

Overall Takeaways

Perhaps some overall takeaways for me? Develop intellectual property where it makes sense, stay focused in areas I'm passionate about, and be more politically aware. Knowing when to get out is also important.

Action Step: What are your Three Highest Value Activities?

Base this on your Future Orientation, your own definition of success, analysis of what the most successful people are/were doing in your various roles, jobs, and anything else that makes sense.

Three is a good but somewhat arbitrary number. You may want two or four or more, but ten or twenty are far too many to focus on.

Of course your highest value activities may change, and change significantly over time. Today, for me, these are my highest value activities in no particular order.

▶ Taking The Infosec Rock Star Project forward.
▶ Working on classes (Intellectual Property): writing/improving/updating, and related material like books, videos, etc.
▶ Teaching classes I'm passionate about.

I kept my list to three. I was very tempted to add something about my ongoing consulting work, and that would have made the top three list last year, and it is number four now.

Notice I didn't list some things that seem like they should be on the list, such as staying current in Infosec. While critical, it flows mostly automatically from the three highest value activities I have listed.

What do these three have in common? They all focus on delivering value. Passion is a common thread, although admittedly more for the first and the third. The first and second have to do with generating Intellectual Property (IP). We will talk much more on IP in a forthcoming section, both traditional IP as defined by law and well beyond.

But I'm an Employee

What if you are an employee? You can't just unilaterally decide what your three highest value activities are and focus on them.

Discuss what you believe to be the highest value activities with your boss. You may want to ask for input first based on what you know about your boss. Come to an agreement on your highest value activities. Perhaps document it in an email.

There will rarely initially be one hundred percent agreement. You will need to have a discussion, and to some extent you might be negotiating with your boss. We will discuss negotiations a bit later, but this is much more of a conversation instead of formal negotiation. This is not a one-time thing; you'll need to update this understanding periodically with your boss.

You may also want to discuss what these highest value activities are with your spouse, your co-workers, and more.

When I had employees in the past, I would periodically ask them what they thought their highest value activities were and the most important things they did.

What they believed were the highest value and what I believed were the highest value almost never initially intersected one hundred percent. Often there was wide divergence.

If your boss and you agree on your highest value activities, you will tend to receive enormous support for what you say no to; saying no to less valuable activities gives you more time to devote to your highest value activities.

What you do and What you don't do are Equally Important

Since there is never enough time to do everything, what you choose to do and what you choose not to do are equally important. This is referred to as opportunity cost in economics but is applicable to many fields. Of course with some things you will have no choice; you need to do them. It doesn't matter if you are a full-time employee, a minion, a contractor, self-employed, or something else. (See the bonus at http://infosecrockstar.com/bonuses/ for the advantages and disadvantages of being a fulltime employee, contractor, and consultant). Some things just need to be done.

With other things, regardless of your role, you will have choices. I often think, "What if I never did this, would it matter?" Some seemingly important things might, in fact, not be important. Perhaps they were very important at some time. Maybe you can just skip them or perhaps delegate them elsewhere.

Sometimes you have to say no; you simply cannot say yes to everything and actually do everything.

Of course, the order in which you do things also matters. It almost seems to be human nature to procrastinate. Don't procrastinate on the most important things. You can put off the less important and not currently time-sensitive items instead.

It is worth analyzing some activities with Zero Based Thinking (and for some this might not apply). Zero Based Thinking is the concept that if you weren't already doing it, would you start doing it today?

The "Not To Do" List

What are you *not* doing on purpose?

One critical concept is the "Not To Do List," whether it is a formal list or not, what are you *not* doing? Often these are things you used to do that are not worth doing anymore, or that someone else can do.

Every time you say yes to something you implicitly say no to something else.

Since you can't do everything, is it important you do not try. What you don't do is as important as what you try to do. Are there things you are doing that you can delegate, ignore, outsource, etc.?

These may be things that were once important but no longer are.

In my case, some of this is as simple as having an accountant to handle some of my finances. I also outsource some graphics, Search Engine Optimization, and editing work. Doing things that I can outsource for under $100 per hour, sometimes $10 per hour, makes no sense. What is your time worth?

What things do you do now, that if it they were never done, would not matter? Stop doing them.

There are a few things, some of which actually made me money, that I have simply stopped doing. Why? There are more valuable uses for my time.

What do you do now that someone else could do adequately, whether it's a coworker, an employee, or someone on Fiverr.com? Notice I did *not* say "do perfectly" or "do as well as you."

The more "less important" things you stop doing, the more important things you can do – duh!

Power of a Positive "No"

- NO – I do not have the time to do the great job it requires.
- Great, but *not* me – I'm not the best person to do this.
- I'd love to, but . . .

Not only do you not have time to do everything, but you can't do everything well. As you become more important, more valuable, more wanted, your time still remains constant at twenty-four hours a day. And your need for sleep doesn't decrease.

Remember, every time you say yes to something, you are implicitly saying no to other things.

When asked to do something, consider the following:

Is it strategic? If it is not on the path to your goals, your success, in tune with your Future Orientation, maybe you shouldn't be doing it. For example, I turned down writing a column for *Success* magazine my literary agent was trying to talk me into. Not only did I not feel qualified, but it wasn't something I saw as strategic.

Are you the right person to do it? Maybe you are not. Maybe someone else can do it better/easier/faster/etc. For example, financials are not a strong point for me. When I've been early in a startup, I've wanted a good financial person in place quickly.

Is it something you can do a great job at? If you are only capable of doing (what my father would call) a "half-assed" job, you shouldn't do it. I'm *not* saying you shouldn't take on projects that stretch your capabilities, because you should, but perhaps, I should not write a compiler, manage a team of salespeople, or open a wine store (although that sounds pretty cool!).

Do you have the time to do it? "I'd love to but I do not have enough time to do a great job," has a nice ring to it sometimes. Will doing it take time away from other things you are doing possibly causing a substandard performance? I'd love to dive headfirst deeper into forensics, but no way do I have the time to do it right.

No is a Complete Sentence

Sometimes you do *not* need to say why. That often gets into discussions on *How* instead of *No*.

Sometimes you can just say no without explanation. Remember that *No* is a complete sentence.

Of course, sometimes you have no choice. You might be the logical person to do it among a group of bad choices. You might need to take one for the team.

"The difference between successful people and really
successful people is that really successful people say no to
almost everything."
-Warren Buffet

Warren Buffett is a very smart guy, and very rich. Of the two hundred countries listed by the United Nations, he has more money than sixty-seven of their combined gross domestic products (GDP).

And he made all the money himself. He didn't make it the old-fashioned way, inheriting or stealing it. (As Foghorn Leghorn would say, "That's a joke, son.")

Action Step: Considering your personal "Future Orientation," what do you currently do that you should not do? Why?

Quickly list some items that you should consider skipping either now or in the near future.

Focus on higher level activities and plans, instead of lower level items like "buy stamps" or "fold underwear" for this exercise.

Remember, if you are a full-time employee then your boss has something to say about this too. We have discussed this in this chapter already.

Here are some things I'm currently not doing.

1) I have some self-study Infosec materials for CPAs. They pay royalties, which do not currently amount to much. I am not the original author, and they both need very little maintenance and deserve a complete rewrite. I'm not updating them right now.

2) I have a number of websites, both security and non-security related. They do make money, sometimes $10K+ a year, although lately a bit less, from advertising and more. I'm letting some domains expire and leaving some others alone that have evergreen content. I've said no to spending time on these websites, even though they make me some passive income.

3) There is a class I teach and until recently I was in charge of managing and updating part of the class. It's undergoing a complete rewrite, as technical classes need periodically. I'm not part of the update team, am not following the work that they are doing, and am not committing to teaching the class in the future. I've said "no" as I don't have enough time. Once the rewrite is done I may reconsider, but it's "no" at least for now!

Clearing Your Mind

The short-term part of the mind is like DRAM, Dynamic Random Access Memory. For example, the laptop I am typing on right now has eight gig of main memory, which is DRAM. That's a lot of memory, but it needs to be refreshed every few milliseconds because it decays over time. Some data is much more efficiently stored in different types of storage, such as a hard drive.

Analogously, your mind can store a lot of short-term information, but it needs to be constantly refreshed. Your mind is not designed to effectively store lots of short-term information. Ever wake up in the middle of the night and suddenly remember something you need to do the next day, or remind yourself of something while brushing your teeth? That is your mind refreshing pieces of short-term information. There are better places to store much of this short-term information.

Your mind can't focus on many things at one time. *Free your mind.* Unclutter your mind. You free your mind by removing "stuff" from it that is better stored elsewhere.

Write it down and at least loosely organize it. Use lists for that purpose.

Lists (Are Mentally Liberating)

Some people have a mental aversion to lists because they believe they might stifle their free spirit and creativity. In reality, lists are mentally liberating. They free up your mind for more important things.

> *"Always work from a list."*
> – Brian Tracy

You'll have multiple lists, depending on whatever works for you, e.g. daily/weekly/monthly/project and perhaps a "someday/maybe" list.

You can track your lists however you want, ranging from electronically, perhaps online or on your phone, good old paper and pen, or even write them on your hand if you prefer. Whatever works for you is fine.

The "Daily To Do" List

Most people use a "Daily To Do List" which needs to be short, perhaps five to seven things maximum. If it has fifteen you will not finish them all, and often will *not* do the most important, which are usually not the fastest or easiest.

Similarly, if you give an employee fifteen things to do, they will not finish them. It's unlikely they will complete the ones *you* consider most important either.

Some of these items might be quickly completed, some might take longer, some might be of unknown duration. Often I will put something similar to "Spend one hour on XXYZ" and schedule a specific time. See time blocking, coming up soon.

Productivity consultant David Allen prefers a "Next Actions List" coupled with putting items that need to be done on specific days directly on your calendar.

Personally I like this "Daily To Do List" to be on paper and visible. Electronic is fine but can easy be lost under other windows if you're not careful about intentionally checking it.

Whatever works for you is fine. I tend to use a combination of paper and pen and my cell phone for lists.

Do the Most Important Item First

So you've got maybe five most important things to do. They are on your "Daily To Do" list and all are critically important.

What do you do first? What you feel like? What you think you can finish easily? What will make your coworker Mary happy?

Do what is *most important* first.

You might think there are five critical things you must do, but guess what? You might only do two of them. You might only do one. Something unexpected might (and often does) happen, so do the most important first. Your "To Do" list may be short, but you might never finish it. Who knows what may happen!

Corollary: What you decide to do next is the most important decision you make!

Other Lists

Without even going into things like grocery lists, you will benefit from having additional lists. You can organize these however works best for you.

For example, besides "Daily To Do" or "Next Action" Lists, many people have Weekly Lists, Monthly Lists, a Someday/Maybe List, and Project Lists.

Some information may be on your calendar as well, and added to your lists as appropriate.

What matters is that you get the info out of your head, not the specific types of lists you use.

You can also have longer term lists, sort of like a life time bucket list. Perhaps you want to write a book someday, surf in Hawaii, start a company, or meet the Coptic Pope (an amazing man!). Write these things down and you'll have a better chance of accomplishing them.

Time Blocking

What is the most important thing for you to do at this point in your life, your career, your whatever (it should be on a list!)? Is there one thing that is the most important? If so, it is a prime candidate for time blocking. Plan some time blocks for the most important thing(s). What is most important right now?

A time block is essentially a meeting with yourself.

Like all successful meetings, a time block needs a specific agenda stating what you are going to do, a specific start and end time, and follow up action items—what you are going to do next. What you do next might be simple like checking an item off your list as done.

Time blocking can span weeks and longer. A friend of mine is working on a book proposal, and has two regularly scheduled blocks of time, Monday and Wednesday from 6-8 a.m. He has kids and a fulltime job, but he can carve that time out for something so important to him.

Setting up time blocks may involve negotiations with a spouse, your boss, or coworkers.

Part of having a successful meeting is scheduling it somewhere free of interruptions. The same applies to time blocking. If you work in a cube in a hectic, interruption driven environment, you might need to go elsewhere during your time blocks. Ignore distractions by turning off your phone, email, Twitter, and Facebook, as appropriate.

As I write this, I am in a time block dedicated to working on this chapter, and am writing in a coffee shop I know is quiet at this time of day and a great environment for me in which to write.

I apply simple time blocking within a day and only to high-priority tasks. For example, throughout the next two weeks I have blocks of time I've dedicated to finishing this book, to taking an online class on leadership, and to working on a business initiative.

Some people, like my friend The Major, apply time blocking to the longer range. For example, I've seen him block out entire weeks and up to months for specific tasks. Others time block their entire days, scheduling something every hour. I do neither. Maybe I'm just not that organized, or maybe I don't need to be, probably some combination of the two. I do what works for me and you need to do what works for you.

Side note: Time blocking works better earlier in the day for most people, even those of us who consider ourselves night owls.

Many highly successful people use time blocking as a significant part of their time management. Have you ever noticed how successful people not only get a lot done, but get the right things done? You want to be doing the right things during your time blocks.

Projects and The Project List

So what is a *project*? Definitions of *project* vary, however there is general agreement that a project has multiple steps and a specific goal or desired outcome. When that goal or outcome is reached, the project is over.

Here are some definitions of projects:

- ▸ "a temporary endeavor undertaken to create a unique product, service or result." – Project Management Institute
- ▸ "a planned piece of work that has a specific purpose (such as to find information or to make something new) and that usually requires a lot of time" – Merriam-Webster
- ▸ "a collaborative enterprise, involving research or design, that is carefully planned to achieve a particular aim" – Wikipedia

We can have formal projects with traditional project management, as well as projects with little to less formal project management. As a general rule, projects with more people involved benefit greatly from formal project management. For projects you are doing yourself, or perhaps you and another person or two, some structure is still enormously helpful. However, full project management might neither be needed nor desired.

The Project List

A project list is simply a list of projects (using a loose definition of projects) you are involved with. Some small projects may only involve you. Your project list is critical to avoid losing track of projects. It's often a simple spreadsheet.

Having a list of all projects can be very useful, with the project name, state of the project, and any other information you deem useful. They are particularly good to make sure any personal projects are not abandoned accidentally.

Traditional Project Management

Traditional Project Management, as defined by The Project Management Institute, consists of five stages. Great project management (and a great project manager) is essential for larger projects.

I may say *traditional project management*, however despite the fact that humans have done project management for millennia, formal project management and project management as a profession didn't appear until the mid-twentieth century.

▸ **Initiation** – determining the nature and scope of the project and whether to go forward
▸ **Planning** - planning time, cost and resources adequately to estimate resources required and manage risk during execution
▸ **Executing** – following the plan
▸ **Monitoring and Controlling** – keeping the plan on track as "no plan survives contact with reality"
▸ **Closing** – formal acceptance, administrative activities, and ending the project

Formal project management absolutely has its place, and we can use more great and classically trained project managers, like Project Manager Institute Certified Project Management Professionals, or PMPs, with years of solid experience.

But not all projects (using our working definition) need this, so if you are a PMP, rest assured that I have plenty of respect for you, but don't get uptight at what's to come.

Smaller projects, such as ones with a small team, perhaps just you, are often handled very differently.

Small Informal Project Approaches

Here are three possible approaches. I certainly didn't invent these or come up with these concepts, although I have found them very useful at times.

The Salami Approach: Break the project into sequential, detailed steps like slices of salami and get started. Pick a slice and complete it.

The Swiss Cheese Approach: Just dive in and do something; start working on the project. In other words, do something, anything. Imagine the project as a big block of work and you are boring holes into it, getting things done, and making progress. This is a great technique when it is not clear what the best way is to get started.

Both the Salami and the Swiss Cheese approaches are great techniques to develop forward momentum.

The Next Step Approach

Sometimes only the next step is obvious or logical. You do the next step, maintaining (or establishing) momentum, and then see what happens.

Example: The Infosec Rock Star Project

When I decided to give my first Infosec Rock Star talk, I had no idea what the next step would be or even if there was a next step. Of course I had plenty of ideas. We always have ideas. I was thinking possible videos, courses, books, etc., but each next step depended on the results of the previous step. There was no clear cut or obvious plan at all.

I didn't know how far I would proceed, how much interest there'd be, or if the feedback would be positive. I began by giving a one-hour talk.

▶ First Step: Give Infosec Rock Star talk.

The talk went well. My audience was very engaged, enthusiastic, and feedback was almost all positive. One person didn't get it, and complained the talk wasn't technical, despite it being billed as not technical and my beginning with the statement that it was perhaps the first one hundred percent non-technical talk I had ever given. You can't please everyone and I don't even care to try.

▸ Next Step(s): Improve, enhance, and give talk multiple times again.

Since the talk was a success, I gave it several times over the next few months, each time evolving it based on input and feedback.

▸ Next Step: Put up website.

I put up a website, and since InfoSecRockStar.com was available it was a no-brainer. I wrote a couple of articles a day building the site up in the process. I had plenty of content and interest.

▸ Next Step: Build an email list: Write e-book from talk and give away in exchange for email addresses. In the next step I decided to build an email list of interested people. Instead of simply asking for people to give me their email address, I decided to write an e-book from my talk and website material and give it away in exchange for an email address. An email list is incredibly powerful and I use it to send visitors my videos, new articles, and more focusing on providing value to the subscribers. Without this email list, the following steps would not have been as successful. If you haven't already, please sign up at InfosecRockStar.com.

▸ Next Step: Make videos.

Next I decided to make a series of three educational videos. Most viewers came from my email list. The videos were a hit so I decided to write a course.

▸ Next Step: Teach Infosec Rock Star Workshop.

My first course was inexpensive and taught entirely live and online. I called it the "Infosec Rock Star Workshop" and told people I would be developing it as I taught it, a week at a time, based enormously on their input. I didn't build the course I thought people wanted, I built the course suggested through extensive surveys of the participants and more.

▶ Next Step: Improve and teach Infosec Rock Star Blueprint.

The next step, a few months later, based on lessons learned, was to launch a new and improved version of the course I called the Infosec Rock Star Blueprint. I "rinsed and repeated," improving the course and teaching it a third time as well online. I taught it in a slightly shorter version, live and in person, at the UK Cyber Academy.

▶ Next Step: Write book. Which you are reading right now.

The next step after this book? I'm not sure yet.

There is a goal, however, and always has been. The goal is to take this to its logical conclusion, whether that is stopping here or building a billion-dollar Infosec Rock Star empire. We will see. I'll keep going forward as long as it makes sense, whether there is a clear path or not.

Why Projects Fail

Unfortunately, many projects fail, either partially or entirely.

The number one reason projects fail is simply scope change. It doesn't matter if it's a project to build something physical, like a bridge or a building, or something non-physical, like software.

Large changes in scope are usually obvious. Small changes, or "scope creep," are not always obvious. Scope creep is sometimes called "requirement creep" or "feature creep." Large projects often have a scope management plan.

Lack or loss of management support is the second reason projects fail. Management support is essential as they control the resources.

Smaller projects sometime fail because they are forgotten or abandoned. An organization is not going to suddenly "forget" about a large plan like constructing new corporate headquarters, searching for a new CEO, or building a new billing system, but a smaller project, one involving a single person or a very few people, might be forgotten. Simply due to the nature of work these days, it might need to be temporarily abandoned. For example, when I'm traveling and teaching back to back six-day/five-night boot camps, many of my projects essentially stop.

Perfection is another big reason for project failure. Nothing is ever perfect, hence nothing can ever be completed to a perfectionist. Good enough is good enough. For example, if I waited for this book to be perfect it would never be done. You wouldn't be reading this now.

Brutal Time Management Tenets

We've talked about how there are more things to do than there is time. As we progress in our careers, in our lives, in our importance, we have even more to do, yet the same amount of time.

Suddenly you may be responsible for more, find yourself in charge of numerous projects, become the defacto resource for a few things or people, or somehow gain a husband/wife/boyfriend/girlfriend who takes up time. There may be children, bosses who need management, or you might have several employees directly reporting to you and more.

Clearly, since time is a very limited resource, we need to manage it, and the most successful folks I know manage their time brutally.

Consider tracking your time for a week; you may be shocked where it goes.

Schedule Your Time or Time will Own You!

Of course, some or much of your work might be interruption driven, but use your schedule. If you do not schedule your time, you risk being primarily reactive instead of proactive.

The level of scheduling is up to you. Mine is somewhat loose. I do not manage my time extremely closely, but that does work and is entirely appropriate for many.

Use whatever method you want: an online calendar, PDA, paper, a physical calendar, etc. Whatever works for you is fine. Almost any time management/scheduling system will also use lists which we have discussed.

I use a physical monthly planner (DayMinder At-A-Glance brand) – pretty old school, but it works for me. Items I enter for specific days cause me to take actions, like make plane reservations, call Bob, add something to a list, sometimes create a new list, etc.

Occasionally Work on the Important but not Time Critical

What is most important or most critical usually has a significant time component to it, at least in our minds. However, you may have extremely important things that have a *mañana* component; they are important, but might never be time critical.

Not everything important is time critical, so occasionally work on the important but not time critical. Schedule time to work on these, or they will never get done. These often have to do with your Future Orientation.

These might include writing a book, or studying for a certification, or something else that brings profit to your career.

Steve Covey's approach to time is similar, yet different. He places tasks into four quadrants. Quadrant IV is the least important, things that are neither urgent nor important. Many people spend by far most of their time in Quadrants I and III. While I is clearly warranted, often things in Quadrant III that are not important may be urgent to others, sometimes because of their poor planning or lack of planning.

It is important we do not ignore Quadrant II tasks; they are important but not urgent. As we said before, they may have to do with your Future Orientation, making them extremely important.

	Urgent	**Not Urgent**
Important	Quadrant I Urgent & Important	Quadrant II Not Urgent & Important
Not Important	Quadrant III Urgent & Not Important	Quadrant IV Not Urgent & Not Important

Avoid Time Vampires

Time Vampire is a term I borrow from master marketer and social engineer Dan Kennedy. He uses the term primarily to refer to people, but the term fits into a more general context: needless energy sapping time wastes.

A Time Vampire may be a committee or task force or whatever that you shouldn't be on. It doesn't mean it isn't important (of course it might be useless too), but perhaps it's not that important to you or someone else would be more effective in that role or . . . A Time

Vampire may be something you do, like checking Facebook or Twitter every five minutes. A Time Vampire might be a person.

There is always someone to waste time with, but some people seem to always waste other people's time. It may be some dolt who stops by and rambles on endlessly about nothing, who everyone tries to avoid. I'm usually able to make some time if a friend or colleague needs a few minutes, but that is a far cry from letting Time Wasting Tom ramble on for forty-five minutes about his Aunt Gretchen and her lumbago.

It might be Luigi from engineering who stops by to talk all the time, says nothing, and seems to never leave. You know, the guy or gal that everyone avoids. "Hey Luigi, I've got a deadline," or "I need to take this call," or you might even fake a call. And if you don't want to lie, well, you can always be blunt and direct instead.

Time Vampires: Email

Email will consume all your time and life if you let it, so don't let it.

Email is the number one Time Vampire for many people.

Always place time limits on email. For example, you may choose to read email from ten to ten-thirty, four to four-thirty, and then a quick check after dinner. If you read email constantly, you'll get very little done except for reading email.

You don't have to answer all your email; no such law nor moral obligation exists. I ignore all spam and semi-spam. Even somewhat legit email will usually get ignored by me if I don't know the sender and if they couldn't be bothered with visiting my site to figure out my name.

Then again, I get several emails from people I've never met who have read my books or read my blogs. I do respond, although sometimes briefly.

I answer a lot of email by telephone. Yes, the telephone still works. Sometimes I'll reply to emails via my cell phone while driving home. Some may dislike this as they want a record of the communications. They can register their complaints with you.

Sometimes I'll answer email in person, such as when my son emails me and I can walk to the next room to see him. I'll also deal with some email with responses like, "Ask me when me meet Friday."

Never respond to short emails with long answers. For example, a one-line question should not elicit a five-page answer; the medium is not designed for exchanges of that sort. I often send one and two word responses, such as "excellent" and "yes," as appropriate.

Now if you're procrastinating anyway, it's ok to read email as it comes in, as well as to respond with long soliloquies if you'd like.

Use Travel/Commute Time

Travel and commute time should not be wasted time.

I do drive a fair amount, although my daily commute is usually from my bedroom to the kitchen table. I return email and phone calls when driving. I listen to security and business podcasts. Lately I've been listening to foreign language lessons in the car. Safety first of course; distracted driving is dangerous.

Basically, my car is a mobile learning lab these days.

As I write this, my commute yesterday was about twenty-seven hours door-to-door (New Hampshire to ten time zones away). Yes, I watched a movie or two, had a drink or two, and fortunately even slept, and I still had hours of time getting great things done. I read a work-related book I was looking forward to digging in to, reviewed/updated some documents, etc., and now I'm on a fourteen hour flight while proofreading and updating.

Reserve Time for Unplanned Events

Even if our jobs and lives are not primarily interruption driven (and yours may be), there will always be unplanned events we will need to deal with. These could be as mundane as the printer or internet dying or as exciting as a fantastic new opportunity arising.

Of course, life also interferes. You or a family member gets sick; your husband or wife has a nervous breakdown; your car has an engine breakdown; you have a mid-life crisis; there is a snow storm (or a sand storm, as I just experienced my first a couple days ago).

Life Balance

Life balance is somewhat of a myth, at least the way people normally think of it.

Many of the most incredible things have nothing to do with life balance. Sometimes we dive in head first and let things balance out afterward in the longer term.

While we can't remotely equate the importance of these two, consider the birth of a child and successfully completing a massive and potentially earthshaking project. Neither of these two have anything to do with (short term) life balance.

I don't distinguish between work and non-work, which of course can be dangerous as it can lead toward becoming a workaholic, which I'm not remotely suggesting. We all have exactly one life. I attempt to fill mine with good things, regardless of whether someone else might categorize them as work or play or something else. As I am self-employed, this is easier for me to say than most. It's also easy for work to take over life, and fortunately I have enough interests in life to prevent that from happening.

You've got one life. Do awesome things.

The Bottom Line

Everything major should flow from Future Orientation, coupled with constant interruptions.

You need a Top Down and Bottom Up approach. Top Down flows from the most valuable activities based on your Future Orientation, and Bottom Up clears *must do* things and interruptions so you can concentrate on the most valuable activities.

Although you should focus on your most valuable activities, expect to get periodically derailed, both by relatively minor things as well as by the major curves life sometimes throws as us.

When this happens, it is your job to get back on track. No one else is going to do this for you, at least not remotely as well as you can for yourself. If you are passionate about what you are doing, and have thought about your Future Orientation, getting back on track is relatively easy.

3

OWN YOUR IMAGE

● ● ● ● ● ● ●

What People Think About You Matters

It would be excellent if we could just focus on doing a great job, focusing on providing value, concentrating on our highest value activities (Future Orientation and the Top Down approach), while handling interruptions that are urgent yet usually far less important things (Bottom Up approach).

That is not how the world works.

What people think about you matters. It's good for people to like you, and it is far more important that people respect you. There are plenty of highly respected people who have been rather unlikeable, who you probably wouldn't enjoy having dinner with other than perhaps for the experience, but who are highly respected nonetheless. Many people disliked Steve Jobs personally. He was often a very harsh individual. But most respected him and gladly followed him. Peter Drucker, an amazing Rock Star of a man often described as "the founder of modern management" was allegedly a very harsh individual. Axl Rose, an incredibly talented man widely respected for his musical skills, appears to be nearly impossible to work with and hence not very likeable by his band mates and others. "He was either childlike, or a dog from hell," [8]says Vicky Hamilton, who managed Axl and his band Guns N' Roses before they were famous.

Respect gives you enormous flexibility and plenty of opportunities.

If the Rolling Stones, enormously respected for their musical talent and more, want to tour, they can. If they want to make another album, they can. If they tour, they can play pretty much anywhere they want. They could even record an album of something absurd like Reggae-Disco-Funk and it would sell. And if critics panned it they could just laugh. Or they could just relax as they have no financial concerns.

The living members of Led Zepplin, another enormously respected band, were offered eight-hundred million dollars for a reunion tour by Richard Branson. They declined. Obviously they can do what they want.

Closer to home, we can probably safely say that Linus Torvalds doesn't worry about money or finding exciting work. He's worth several million and is also funded by a foundation. Although he is not without controversy, we probably all think he is pretty cool and he has earned massive respect.

The Rolling Stones, Led Zepplin, and Linus Torvalds have a lot in common. They are widely respected, they have great images, their reputations proceed them, and more. This gives them enormous flexibility to do what they want, whether it is another great thing or relaxing for a while. They have lots of opportunities and lots of choices. Although some might argue this is because they have lots of

---

8   Davis, Stephen. *Watch You Bleed: The Saga of Guns N' Roses*. Los Angeles: Gotham Press, 2008. Print.

money, having money is a side effect of the great respect they have earned.

What Do People Think of You?

So, what do people think of you? You might be very surprised. People's self-image is often very different than others image of them. Why not ask a few people and find out?

Now, if you ask people in person they might feel they need to give an immediate answer, putting them in an awkward position. You might word it differently than "What do you think of me?" which can make people uncomfortable. Still, it can be awkward to confront people in the hall or the phone or somehow else in real time and seemingly demand their opinion of you, and the answers you get may not be very accurate.

If you ask via email these people can think for a while and you are more likely to get an honest answer. I'll also suggest you ask people who know you more than just a little. An answer from someone you have known for fifteen years is more valuable than someone you have known for fifteen minutes, although both may be valuable.

I asked a few people who have known me a while, both professionally and personally, by sending an email asking, "What do you think my top personality quirks or traits are?"

In total I emailed six people and five answered. One email address may have been old. They ranged from college and grad school friends I've been in touch which through the years, as well as people I've worked with. I made sure to ask both technically-oriented and nontechnical people, males and females, a diverse group.

Action Step: So what do people think of you? Let's find out!

Email several people who know you, asking: "What do you think my top personality quirks or traits are?"

What I got back:

Looking at commonalities, apparently I am an intelligent, outgoing, and fun eccentric. I did think I would get a lot of "hard working" and "technical" type responses, but I did not. I was prepared to be surprised.

The outgoing surprised me as I am a classic introvert. I am quite social but definitely an introvert.

The eccentric was not a surprise. Fortunately, as a technical person we are given a lot of latitude to be somewhat strange or eccentric by society, just as we expect Rock Stars to be "out there."

Branding

In the above exercise, when people asked me why I was asking, "What do you think my top personality quirks or traits are?" I answered, "Branding exercise." What's a brand and branding and why do we care?

A *brand* is a promise. It's what people think about something. It's the core without all the details. There is safety and consistency in brands. A brand is what prevents something from being a commodity.

Personal branding is, you guessed it, branding applied to you. It describes what's special and unique about you and why you are not a commodity.

Rock Stars have strong brands. They are not commodities. Each Rock Star is unique and there is no replacement. There is only one

Mick Jagger, one Lady Gaga, one Linus Torvalds, one Axl Rose, one Steve Jobs, one Madonna.

You do *not* want to be a commodity. Commodities are inexpensive. They are replaceable. Commodity, i.e. generic, does not garner much respect, if any at all.

You are a brand. Your personal brand is who you are.

Your personal brand will help attract the right people, organizations, and opportunities, as well as repel those that are inappropriate for you. A brand cannot appeal to everyone; that just doesn't work.

For example, my twenty-something nephew Gregory Peccary just showed up with long hair and an unkempt shaggy beard, looking for a place to crash while following the bands Dead & Company and Phish. Grandma, of course, commented on his hair, and he replied that it attracted the right people and repelled uptight, annoying people. Yup, although appearance is only one part of a brand, this is personal branding in action.

Rock Stars have strong brands. They are not just a cog in the machine. You can't just replace one Rock Star with another.

Some Well Known Brands

Starbucks – strong coffee and a comfortable place to sit

I go to Starbucks regularly. At Starbucks I know I will get fresh and strong coffee and a comfortable place to sit. The place down the street may have better coffee, but I don't know. Starbucks is a safe choice. Down the street I may get weak and stale coffee.

I don't love Starbucks coffee by any means. Some coffee nerds will tell you it is downright horrible, they roast most of the character out of the beans, and they are not sticklers on bean roasting date freshness. Lots of places might make coffee that is several orders of magnitude better. I still go to Starbucks often. I never buy Starbucks coffee beans to make at home as there is plenty of coffee I prefer enormously more. But their brand is comfortable and dependable.

Harley-Davidson – freedom

Yes, they sell motorcycles, but the brand is about freedom. It is not about transportation or noisy, two-wheeled machines, it's about lifestyle, a lifestyle of freedom. It is such a strong brand that people tattoo the Harley-Davidson's logo onto their bodies.

Volvo – safety

I drive a Volvo. I used to drive a Porsche, but it somehow sank, and fine German engineering doesn't do well when submersed in salt water. Now, especially with little kids, safety is far more important. Is a Volvo really the safest car? I really have no idea, having done very little research. I wanted an extremely safe car so I bought a Volvo. Its brand, its promise, is safety, so I just went and bought one.

Rolls Royce – the best

It's been a long time since I was in a Rolls Royce, and although it is a very nice car, is it the best? I'd probably rather have a Bentley, all things being equal, but we accept a Rolls Royce as being the best. The CEO of one of my large clients often says his company is the Rolls Royce of his industry. He doesn't mean his company resembles a mode of transportation; he means it is *the best*, and it is priced accordingly and employees are urged to do whatever possible to make it the best.

You - ???

What do people think of you? You can guess, and maybe be right, or ask a few people as in the action item above.

Branding & Authenticity

"I yam what I yam and that's all what I yam."
- Popeye the Sailor Man

Popeye the Sailor Man is a fictional cartoon character who has appeared in comic strips, animated cartoons, and even a movie starring Robin Williams.

Popeye has a clear brand: Honest, brave, dependable, and loyal. Simple, yet not stupid. Uneducated and lacking manners, although capable of devising creative solutions to problems.

Although he had good qualities and knew it, Popeye knew he was a simple, uneducated, uncultured sailor as well. He was authentic. There is no way he could have pretended to be educated, cultured, a connoisseur of fine wines, or a rancher from Montana for long. Sure, he could have faked it for little while, but just for a little while.

> *"You can fool all the people some of the time, and some of*
> *the people all the time,*
> *but you cannot fool all the people all the time."*
> -Abraham Lincoln

We absolutely have some control of our brand, but it has to be true to who we are. It needs to be authentic. For example, I couldn't pretend that I was a super-conservative-everything-by-the-book-guy for long, although I am rather conservative in many ways. I have a creative edge that comes off at times as eccentric and that is a core part of me. I certainly have some control of it, and act more restrained when I am getting to know someone initially. As the saying goes, "You don't open the kimono all at once." When you first interact with someone, you want to reveal your authentic self, but not necessarily all of it at once.

Brands Invoke Strong Feelings

A good brand attracts as well as repels.

You want to attract the right people, the right "fans," as well as repel the wrong people. Repel may be too strong a word in many cases, but not always.

For example, ISIS is certainly attracting a lot of people. You need an extremely strong brand to get tens of thousands of people from other countries to travel to a war zone to fight as they have. They certainly repel a lot of people too, presumably most people.

Is this Brand Consistent?

Consistency is important in branding.

There is a storage place near me that advertises itself as "Creative." I'm not so sure I want my storage to be creative. Reliable is number one for most people, convenient is good, but *creative*? I don't get it.

Of course I understand wanting to brand themselves and position themselves differently than their competitors to get away from being a commodity. I'm not an expert in the storage business, although I have used storage services, and maybe it works for them. Maybe it gives them a slight edge against their competitors. It is unique and makes them stand out, and that is good.

I know a graphic artist who has a cat on her business card. When I asked her about it, she simply said that she loved cats. What does that have to do with graphic arts? In this case, the cat was essentially a non sequitur and not consistent with her brand.

I also know a personal trainer who smokes a couple packs of cigarettes a day, often stepping out of the health club where they work and visibly smoking. Very inconsistent.

How about a former US Marine incident handler who cultivates a macho image and has light pink business cards? Again, inconsistent.

A brand needs to be consistent across all its "touch" points—everywhere a customer or potential customer interfaces with the brand. And remember, you are a brand and you have customers, just like everyone does. Your customers are the people you serve, whether they are internal customers, external customers, or whether money ever exchanges hands. We all serve and support others. These others are our customers.

Is your brand consistent across all the touch points where the people you serve interface with you? Strong brands are consistent.

Positioning

Positioning is the position something or someone holds in people's minds.

The concept of positioning comes from the highly recommended and groundbreaking classic, *Positioning, The Battle for your Mind*, by Al Ries and Jack Trout; a fun and easy read, despite being a slightly but amusingly dated book.

Positioning Examples:

- Coca Cola – part of everyday life
- Keith Richards – drugs and rock and roll
- Subway – fresh healthy food (as opposed to traditional fast food)

Branding and positioning are highly related. You'll even hear the term *brand positioning*, but they are somewhat different. If you'd like, feel free to search online and read for hours about people's opinions on branding versus positioning.

Rather than potentially endless and at times very interesting debates, here is an example based on Coke. We do not claim it is a perfect example, and the inevitable person from Coca Cola may want to debate the fine points or even the coarse points.

Brand/Positioning Example: Coca Cola

The main consumers of Coca Cola are essentially everyone between twelve and thirty years old, so Coca Cola needs to appeal primarily to this group.

Brand: fun, joy, happiness

Although we could also add "refreshing and thirst quenching" if we wanted, the brand is not foremost about being a beverage.

Positioning: Coca Cola is positioned as a part of everyday life, having a good time with friends and family

Think of all the Coca Cola ads you have seen throughout the years. It is positioned as a part of everyday life and shown in situations in which people are enjoying themselves with friends and family.

Positioning is Extremely Difficult to Change

Keith Richards is one of the best rock and roll guitar players ever and hasn't had a drug arrest since the '70s. Still, he is stuck with the "drug" moniker. Think Keith Richards, think drugs and rock and roll. Maybe he's been clean since the late '70s? I doubt it as do most people, but it doesn't matter.

> *"I've never had a problem with drugs. I've had problems with the police."*
> – Keith Richards.

Changing Positioning...Slowly

Changing positioning takes consistency over a long time period. Time is on your side and patience is required, however it may not be practically possible as well. Sometimes, as the saying goes, "You can't get there from here."

Changing what people think of you, or security, or anything else, may be possible in your organization, but it requires consistency and time.

You need patience, but not too much patience. It sometimes is impossible to change the position something or someone holds in people's minds. Just like a baby duck may imprint on a dog and decide it is its mother, a position in one's mind may be near impossible to change.

For example, I'm a consultant and I know if I go into a company working for human resources or training, I will never work directly with executives. It's just not going to practically happen. If, however, I start working at the higher levels of an organization, my position in the executives' minds is that I'm a smart guy on par with them. If I start as a "training guy" or with human resources, and everyone seems to hate human resources, especially executives in my experience, I stay there in their minds.

Sometimes it may be time to move on to where you can form a new first opinion, or perhaps where security is respected or even just less hated.

If Volvo started building amazing sports cars that blew away Porsches, Ferraris, and Lamborghinis, would they sell? It would be a hard sell. Volvo is associated with safety and sports cars are absolutely not!

If Coca Cola started making kickass whiskey, would people buy it? Probably not. Trying to portray whiskey like Coca Cola, as a part of everyday life, would not go over well. There might even be protests that Coca Cola was encouraging alcohol abuse or similar.

People Get What They Expect
This is one reason positioning is so hard to change.

"The project was late" vs. "Ted messed it up"

There are organizations I consulted with where I could do no wrong. If anything went wrong, it was assumed to be because of the conditions or someone else; never me. There was also an organization in which I was originally associated with a "very troubled project," and that troubled project haunted me well after it was over. If a project had problems, people thought, "Well, Ted's projects always screw up." Forget logic here; I was thrown at failing projects, which was my role, so of course some projects had failures (as well as successes).

Picasso vs. Some Unknown Artist

Imagine taking a piece of art from a famous artist, and slapping a "Smith" or "Jones" on it. Most people won't like it as much if "Smith" or "Jones" painted it than if a famous artist like Picasso or Monet did.

Dom Perignon vs. Some Unknown Champagne

There are lots of phenomenal Champagnes available, and many have very different tastes; personal preferences matter a lot!

Still, to someone who knows nothing about Champagne, a famous brand like Dom Perignon or Cristal impresses. They are much more likely to like it than some equally good or better Champagne that they have never heard of.

People do get what they expect; this makes positioning so hard to change.

Positioning/Branding in Security

What people think about security in your organization matters. If people think horrible things, well, perception is reality, or at least limited reality, and hopefully we can improve that. And keep in mind that what people think about security affects what people think about you by extension.

In security we are basically pushing something almost no one wants. This has challenges.

Ideally the brand includes elements of smart people who add value to the organization, and "helpful" and "easy to work with," or at least not "totally annoying to deal with."

Hopefully the position is stronger than "a necessary evil." Certainly something like "making compliance straight forward" or "enabler of services" is much better.

I'm not sure what brand or positioning security has in your organization or what it should have as every organization is different, but hopefully it is positive. It isn't always. If it isn't, it may be a long uphill road to get there and include the need for a lot of patience and consistency over time. As long as things are trending upward I am happy. Improvement may be slow, but many worthwhile changes are.

5 Levels to Rock Star

In chapter one we introduced the five levels to Rock Star. Let's look at those in more detail now.

Rock Star is a progression. It is something we work toward, and when we attain it, we can always still improve—as well as fade away. I've divided the progression to Rock Star into five basic levels. Just like the seven OSI networking layers, where seven isn't magical (they could have picked five, eight or ten layers and subdivided the functionality differently instead), five levels are not magical either.

They are just a convenient framework for discussion.

Rock Star	**Specialist:** This is where you Rock!
Authority	This is your area of authority
Expert	This is your area of expertise
Stable	This is what you do
Survive	**Generalist:** You will do anything. You need work!

Notice as you move up the levels, you go from generalist to specialist. If you are right out of school and need a job, or just lost your job and need to pay the mortgage and feed your kids, you will take almost any job. If you are a Rock Star, like Madonna, you do your own music plus anything else you want; you're a Rock Star and can do what you want within reason.

Survive:

At the Survive level, you need a job or perhaps have a job of some sorts that simply doesn't rock. It may be a fine job for a while. For example, maybe you're working at the help desk and learning a lot fast.

Stable:

At the Stable level, you've got a good job. Hopefully you like it, or at least most parts. It pays well. If you lose it, you can probably find another one but there may be a lot of effort involved.

We do need to note that many people are at the Stable level and extremely happy and content. They have great lives. Some people even bounce between Survive and Stable and are quite content. However, since you are reading this, chances are you aspire to more.

(Recognized) Expert:

At the Expert level, you have developed expertise, which happens naturally over time and with usually some pretty hard work. You not only have expertise just like those at the Stable and Survive levels might, but you are recognized for your expertise. You are a recognized expert. Maybe you are an occasional speaker in your area of expertise or have authored something; basically, you have created goodwill and visibility somehow and are recognized for it. We will talk about techniques for doing this later.

At the Expert level and above, the concepts of employee, contractor, and consultant merge somewhat and continue to converge as we move on to Authority and Rock Star because you simply have more choices, along with higher pay.

More at

http://infosecrockstar.com/bonuses/ on the differences and benefits of the employee, consultant, and contractor models.

If you are an employee, perhaps at an organization you love and hope to stay at forever, you are well remunerated and starting to develop a lot of choice over projects and positions within your organization. Don't be surprised, though, if at this level and above, you get some gentle pressure to dive into messy projects that are having trouble, just like sometimes I get the, "Hey, what are you doing, Ted? Can you get on a call or on a plane today?" call from friends and colleagues when they have a problem.

You are trusted and even very capable of handling messy situations that most others simply can't.

Hopefully you have developed or are developing some non-geek skills like communication and basic self-direction and leadership, which are helpful for anyone, but will be necessary as you continue to approach Rock Star.

Authority:

An Authority is a widely regarded and respected expert and in addition, has innovative ideas and opinions.

Others terms that are sometimes used include: Leading Expert, Expert among Experts, Thought Leader, Go to Guy/Gal. I like the term *Thought Leader*, but it's become horribly overused these days and its meaning has become diluted, so we'll stick with *Authority* for now.

What distinguishes an Authority from any old Expert is some combination of innovative ideas, learned opinions, and perhaps intellectual property. For example, if I need help with International Tax Law because I'm based in the US and do pen testing internationally, any competent US based international law specialist should be an expert and capable of helping me.

If, however, the US is enacting new international tax laws, almost certainly horrifically complex, your average expert will be of limited use. An Authority or *Thought Leader* (yup, I used the term) in the area of international taxation is what I want. They will have opinions and insight.

At this level your non-geek skills like communication and self-direction and leadership have improved substantially.

Rock Star:

A Rock Star is an authority, plus a lot more.

This "a lot" more can be broken into two categories.

The first, and simplest, is that a Rock Star is simply better known. I'll use the term *celebrity*. You can even to some extent create this celebrity out of almost nowhere, although to be and remain credible, you better have serious skills. Perhaps you could hire a Public Relations firm to draw publicity or run advertisements promoting yourself. We will not be talking much about tactics like these.

You may or may not remember the musical group Milli Vanilli, incredibly popular in the late '80s and early '90s, who won a Grammy award and then had it stripped, because they did not actually sing their own songs. The perpetrators of this scam, not the two poor saps on stage, almost pulled it off if it hadn't been for a technical glitch during an MTV performance in which the music kept skipping and repeating. Yes, Geek is essential! And they screwed up Geek-wise as well as ethically! Fake (and short lived) Rock Stars.

The second is that a Rock Star is an Authority *plus* a number of non-geek skills and mindsets that make them far more effective, and can absolutely lead to increased visibility and on to celebrity. Briefly, they include things like self-direction, communication, business understanding, leadership, time management, project management, negotiation, results orientation, and lots more. We have discussed many of these skills and will discuss more as we continue.

So, What's an *Expert* Anyway?

Since Rock Stars, Authorities, and (of course) Experts *are* experts, let's discuss what an Expert is.

The mere concept of what constitutes an expert confuses most people. An expert is "a person with extensive knowledge or ability,"[9] according to Wikipedia, which means they know more than others. It

---

9   "Expert." *Wikipedia*. Wikimedia Foundation, Web. 20 Dec. 2016.

is a relative term. It doesn't mean #1 Expert in the world. It doesn't mean there is nothing else left to learn.

Take these two examples. first, people consider me an expert at cryptography. I even have a couple of math degrees so I can understand the underlying and often very hairy math. I could start talking about crypto with zero preparation or notes and go for hours. I have plenty of practical experience as well as knowledge.

Now compare me with the crypto gurus at the NSA. Sure, I could probably teach the entry level mathematicians they recruit from college a lot, but compared to their world class experts I know little. Yet people legitimately call me an expert in crypto, even though I'm not the #1 (or even remotely #1000) expert worldwide. I am, however, still an expert.

Next example, let's talk about running. Sometimes I like to run, although I do not have a runner's physique and will never be fast. I have run three races in my adult life. Three times I've attempted a half marathon, but never even began the race. The fourth time I succeeded, but that's not important to this discussion, although success is good. The first time I had a massive ankle sprain two weeks before the event, the kind in which the medical professionals tell you "it would be better if you broke it." I was ready but incapable. The second race was cancelled due to a freak snow storm. The third time I stopped training due to a nasty virus, followed by lots of business travel. Yet even before I had started, much less completed a half marathon, to an aspiring half marathoner, someone who has just started thinking about half marathons or even started training, I was an expert of sorts. In fact, a neighbor was planning a half marathon and constantly picked my brain because they considered me an expert. A relative expert of course, but all experts are relative. I had knowledge and experience that was very valuable to them. In fact, I might be a more useful "expert" to a fledgling half-marathoner than a seasoned runner.

Types of Experts

Since now we discussed what an expert is and since Rock Stars, Authorities, and obviously Experts *are* experts, let's discuss expert status a bit more.

There are different types of experts. You can be a world renowned expert, although perhaps you are not comfortable with that. Maybe you don't want to be on the news giving opinions on the latest hack, or quoted in the *Wall Street Journal* and *USA Today*, or maybe your employer isn't comfortable with that and you love your job and employer. That is absolutely cool.

You can also be world renowned, but only visible within Infosec. This is certainly easier, and maybe that includes going to and maybe speaking at some of the 'cons.

Maybe you just want expert status in your industry, whether that is insurance, or banking, or petrochemicals, or transformer oil, and yes, there is transformer oil industry (I was once interviewed on this topic and the interview was published in seven languages).

There can be and often is a progression, in growing and possibly expanding your expert status if you desire.

The type of Expert you want to be determines your strategy. Speaking, writing, getting press, social media, etc. are just tactics; none are essential, and depending on your strengths and desires some will be more appropriate than others.

Strengthening our Branding/Positioning

Branding and Positioning are so intertwined that we simply are not going to worry about the distinctions between them. If you are further interested, you can spend hours googling and reading online the different and often conflicting ways experts go about defining them.

What is clear is what we want in our brand and positioning at a minimum.

We already talked somewhat about trust. A key element of trust is consistency. A key element of a brand is also consistency. Consistency is important.

We want to be seen as professionals, which comprises several facets we'll discuss.

We also want to be recognized experts. To be recognized we need some visibility.

To be an Authority or Rock Star we also need more. Innovative ideas, opinions, and intellectual property are wonderful for propelling us to the Authority and Rock Star levels, as well as for visibility and getting us to Expert status. We will be cover these.

What's Your Name?

Your name matters because people reference you by your name. Your name matters because people are always looking you up and you want them to find *you*. Your name matters because experts are known by their name and you want to be an expert.

People generally look you up online, and they look you up using the search engines by name.

This includes people you work with, people considering hiring you, other professionals, neighbors, people fantasizing about dating you, and even people thinking about buying a used car from you. Hey, babysitters have Googled me before they would watch my kids. The mailman Googled me since I seem to live such a strange lifestyle (a traveling consultant who throws the occasional wild party).

Unique or Unusual Names are Good

Unique or unusual names are good because they are easy to lookup.

I, Ted Demopoulos, am lucky. So is Seth Godin. Rumpelstiltskin is lucky to have a great name too. Ditto for Moxie CrimeFighter Jillette, the daughter of Penn Jillette of Penn and Teller fame. It is certainly unique, but I'm not sure if I like it.

The good news is you do have some control over your name.

In the USA and many other jurisdictions, you may legally use any name you want as long as it is not with the intention to commit fraud or other crimes. You could even make up a name and use it if you want to. This is perfectly legal in many countries, but because I am not a lawyer I recommend you consult one who can confirm this process.

You could use a variant of your first name.

For example, if Ted Demopoulos was a common name, I could use "Theo" or "Theodore" instead of "Ted" professionally. I could also use the Greek variant of my first name and go by "Theodoros Demopoulos."

You can add a middle name or initial.

"Bob J. Smith" is more unique and easier to look up than "Bob Smith." If Ted Demopoulos wasn't so unusual I could go with "Ted Demetrious Demopoulos."

"Andrew Clay" is a pretty common name but "Andrew Dice Clay" is not. He simply adopted or made up his middle name.

Hey, even Joe Smith could become "Joe B. Smith" or maybe "Joe B.D. Smith"—perhaps "B.D." for his college nickname "Bulldog."

You can totally and legally change your name (in some jurisdictions).

Most people are not going to do this, but it is possible in many countries and there are some extreme examples below, together with some more moderate examples.

Name Change Examples

▶ Todd Smith became "LL Cool J"

▶ David Scott became "David Meerman Scott"

▶ Bill Bailey became "Axl Rose"

▶ Michael Fox became "Michael J. Fox"

▶ Andrew Clay Silverstein became "Andrew Dice Clay"

▶ Bruce Wayne became "Batman"—Oh wait, that's different!

Now, you are probably not going to change your name to "LL Cool J" (It's already taken; sorry.) and you're probably not considering a massive name change, like Muzyad Yakhoob to Danny Thomas or Marion Mitchell Morrison to John Wayne (notice these two are pre-Internet changes to more common names), but you could easily start using a middle name or initial or similar.

And of course, even if you are "Bob Smith" people should be able to find you by googling your name and company or name and place of residence or name and forensics or whatever.

Your Name and Consistency

Do you use multiple names professionally? This includes in your bio or resume (also known as a CV), business cards, email signature, and more.

Maybe your business card says "James Quentin Smith" but everybody calls you Jim (except old friends who maybe call you Jimmy or Jimbo) and your email signature says "James Smith."

If you use multiple names, like James Smith, Jim Smith, Jim Q. Smith, and James Quentin Smith, is there is good reason why? If not, you should probably choose just one and keep it consistent. And don't worry about your old friends.

My name is Ted Demopoulos, not Theodore Demopoulos or Ted J. Demopoulos or Theodore James Demopoulos or Teddie-Bear Demopoulos. Consistency matters.

Sure, my passport and birth certificate might say something slightly different, but I only use "Ted Demopoulos" professionally. I suggest you standardize on one name, unless you have a very good reason not to.

Certifications (and Your Name)

There is no question that certifications are becoming more important. Twenty years ago no one cared about certifications in our field. Ten years ago few, if any, cared. Today, many people care. Whether you are applying for a fulltime job or a consulting gig, often a certification is simply a checklist item; you just need it. I get plenty of government folks in my classes who need to pass the associated certification exam to keep their jobs, or as they sometimes put it, to avoid being "fired or retired."

The top certifications are debatable, but certainly the top vendor neutral certifications include the following:

▶ The CISSP - Certified Information Systems Security Professional. It's been around the longest and hence is the best known and most widely respected.

▶ GSEC - The GIAC Security Essentials Certification. GIAC is Global Information Assurance Certification and is owned by SANS. The other GIAC/SANS certifications are also highly respected.

▶ CISA and CISM - The Certified Information Systems Auditor and Certified Information Security Manager. CISA and CISM are both from ISACA, previously known as the Information Systems Audit and Control Association but now known by its acronym only.

There are plenty of other valuable and respected certifications, including ones focused on certain areas like forensics, pen testing, and vendor specific certifications. This is not remotely an all-inclusive list.

Note that it doesn't matter what you think about various certifications. It matters what others think!

Should you list certifications after your name, essentially as part of your name? That is a question with many opinions. My opinion is that one or a very small number of certifications, assuming they are very well known, can be helpful. Personally I do not, as I'm fairly well established (and my name is already long enough!).

Also, whenever I see a business card that has like a gazillion certifications listed, I tend to think that person is a bozo. Don't take offense at this as some of my friends do this and are not bozos, but I think it looks silly to list piles of obscure and not so obscure initials after your name. People do this in many fields, not just Infosec.

You should absolutely list certifications in other places certainly, like in your CV/resume and on LinkedIn.

This Professional Thing

Professionalism is important. It encompasses several areas, including ethics, appearance, behavior, and responsibility. As technical professionals we are given wider latitude when it comes to this professional thing, certainly far more than accountants or lawyers, although ethics are non-negotiable. This is certainly a good thing, yet we should act *and* look professional.

Ethics

A professional is ethical. People will generally forgive you for making mistakes, but not for being unethical. Unethical people are simply not trusted, and trust is essential.

So what exactly are ethics? Ethics are hard to define and many definitions are circular, but we'll go with "basic concepts and principles of decent human behavior" and "doing what is morally right."

The difficulty with ethics is that not everything is clearly ethical or unethical: there are enormous gray areas. Here are some examples.

You are asked to portray a product or service in a favorable light to a customer. There is nothing wrong with emphasizing the positive, but where is the line between being positive and being unethical? Clearly lying crosses the line. How about omitting some information? What if you are asked difficult questions?

Where does your loyalty lie if there is a conflict between your boss and your organization? Who do you side with?

The president of your company asks you to keep an eye on someone. Perhaps it seems like personal concern as in, "Hey can you keep an eye on Bob? I'm worried about him and hope he's ok. Seems like something is up with him." At what point does this become spying and unethical? What if the president also asked that person to keep an eye on you?

Is it ok to date the boss? A coworker? Someone who directly reports to you? How about the babysitter?

These questions do not always have clear cut answers but demonstrate the gray areas in ethics.

Responsibility

Professionals are responsible.

Being reliable and punctual is part of being professional. If something will be not as expected, let the stakeholders know as soon as reasonably possible.

Deliver when you say you are going to whenever possible. We all know projects are sometimes late, but this should be the exception.

Physical construction projects, things like bridges, buildings, pyramids, and roads, are very often late (and over budget) and we have been doing projects like these for millennia. It should be no surprise that non-physical projects, such as software projects, are also very often late (and over budget).

When something is not on track, tell the stakeholders. Let them know it will be late or over budget or whatever the circumstance is. Telling someone a project will be five months late on the day it is expected is absolutely unprofessional. People hate negative surprises.

Appearance

In some areas, you may have little control over dress and appearance. Although very old school, in some workplaces you are expected to dress in very specific ways. I've worked in offices where all men were expected to wear a suit, white shirt, and tie. As another example, male IBMers traditionally had a jacket and tie uniform, and never a beard.

Generally speaking, dress standards have relaxed in the vast majority of places, and we have much more choice.

I am certainly not going to tell you how to dress, but appearance does matter and it certainly includes how you dress. In particular, if someone hasn't met you before, your appearance is about all they have to form an opinion of you. Your appearance says something about you. It doesn't always say what you think it does.

I always dressed somewhat like a bum. There were entire summers I wore old, ratty t-shirts and aged shorts with dirty sneakers or sandals. I certainly could do this; I can pretty much do whatever I want. I am a low maintenance and casual guy & work for myself. That was apparently not what my appearance said. It seemed to say, "I don't care. I don't care about myself or much of anything else."

I certainly did dress up at times to show respect, like for church or weddings and certainly at customs/immigrations, but it was rare.

A few years ago I started to dress much more nicely. Real shoes that I actually shine. A belt that matches my shoes. Nice shirts with collars. Decent pants, often jeans, that fit appropriately. All my clothes fit. Clothes that didn't fit, ratty t-shirts regardless of their historical significance, and more are gone.

The difference in how people treated me was staggering. I believe I gave off (and still do give off) a, "I'm worth it. I'm valuable enough to take care of myself," vibe.

Historically, the professional rule is if you are not sure, dress one level nicer than the people you are going to meet. Of course there are plenty of exceptions.

What Does Your Appearance Say?

Let's look at some examples:

▶ The guy who shows up for an interview or first date in a ratty t-shirt and worn out shoes

He might think his appearance says he is casual and relaxed, or that his appearance is superficial and doesn't matter, but in reality most people will interpret his appearance as saying, "You're not that important to me." This is generally not the impression you want to give.

▶ The self-made billionaire who attends board meetings in
sandals and shorts

This is a very different scenario than a job interview or first
date. The message here is closer to, "I'm here for my brain." Very
occasionally I have dressed down in similar situations, where my
expertise and experience were being actively courted.

▶ Someone who is reasonably well dressed, groomed, and
fashionable

The general message here is, "I'm worth it. I take of myself
because I'm worth it." I wouldn't have believed this a decade
ago, but it is true.

The focus here is on *reasonably well*, which of course can
have different interpretations in different scenarios. As for
fashionable, fashion is personal and I don't follow trends. No
backward baseball caps or man-buns for me.

▶ Tony from Turkey who stopped shaving and started showing
up in t-shirts when everyone else wore suits

The message here was, "I'm important enough that I can do
what I want," and quite honestly, Tony was.

Your Appearance and Fitting In

I have friends who always look and dress like bikers, as well as
friends who are heavily tattooed and pierced. Some of them work in
our field and some are quite successful as well. I am not asking anyone
to be unauthentic; do your own thing. Once you are an established
Rock Star you can be as outrageous as you want; however, as a general
rule, if your appearance fits in at least somewhat, life is easier.

Also, in Infosec most of us are not known for our style, neatness,
and appearance. People do treat you better when you are better
dressed. Of course you need to apply some common sense here. I
wouldn't go to a biker bar or Grateful Dead concert dressed in a

tuxedo (well, actually, I might; it would be highly amusing—but that's me! I wouldn't recommend it for you).

Would you show up in for a job interview dressed as a mime? I hope not, unless it's for a mime position.

Sexist comment: Gentlemen with no sense of style, go shopping with a woman—but not your mother. If shopping alone, ask women how clothes look. "Do these pants seem to fit me?" "What do you think about this color shirt for me?" You get the idea.

Your Online Appearance

Your appearance includes your online appearance.

It is amazing how many people will look you up online, of course usually by name, and we have discussed the importance of your name already. People you are going to meet professionally, people who hear about you in just about any way, people who are working with you, of course people considering hiring you, and the list goes on. People in my talks Google me, most of my neighbors have Googled me (some of which are convinced I'm a spy; I'm not!), random acquaintances Google me, and I know many of you have Googled me too.

Just as you are hopefully decently dressed and groomed, ideally when someone looks you up online they should find positive things. They had better find something, because if nothing shows up it may be suspicious. Rest assured, if little shows up this is an easy problem to fix.

We do have a lot (although certainly not total) control over what appears when someone types our name into a search engine, or if we have a more common name then perhaps our name and company or name and place we live. Now if you've been accused of embezzling a billion dollars or murdering your butler, whether convicted or not, there will be some bad things about you online and you can't make them go away.

Obviously the offline world is echoed online. The Internet isn't special anymore. It's just a part of ordinary life now. Things in newspapers and other publications, conferences, and more are all online. In fact, as I write this I'm in Brussels teaching a class, and that fact appears online and shows up in a search.

Action Step: Look yourself up online using at least two search engines.

I suggest Google and Yahoo! or Bing. You may need to use your name plus "something" – such as company you work for, job role/title, or where you live if your name is not very unique or if you do not have high visibility online.

For example, if you are "Bob Smith" you may need to add additional descriptors like "Bob Smith Security" or "Bob Smith Boston" or "Bob Smith <company name>".

Look at the first two-three pages and then a deeper page also, maybe page five or ten or twenty.

Hopefully you were able to find yourself. If not, you have some work to do and we'll look at many ways, some very simple and free, to get some visibility.

Is the information accurate? Does it portray you well? Is there any "old stuff" about you that you can take down or have taken down?

If there are horrible things about you online, like you've been accused of running an international drug cartel or you are O.J. Simpson, these horrible things will not go away, but you can at least put up some content telling your side of the story.

Letting the World Know You Rock

Cogs are invisible. Rock Stars are not. Cogs provide minimal value. Rock Stars provide a lot more!

We are going to look at a mix of online, offline, and blended methods to help you achieve expert status and increase visibility and help you move toward Rock Star.

Some of these methods may seem far out, some may not be applicable to you now, and some absolutely will be. Keep an open mind. And be creative here.

But my Job Won't Let Me

There may be some restrictions on what you can do based on where you work. For example, some companies do not want people talking to the press unless explicitly authorized. Some, like the SANS Institute, actively encourage people to talk to the press and identify themselves as working with SANS.

Some companies, such as Apple, are highly secretive and strongly discourage public interaction. Others, like Microsoft, are the opposite. At one point, Microsoft actively encouraged thousands of employees to start openly blogging about their work.

In almost any job, some of what follows will apply. There are some exceptions such as maybe if you are some kind of spy under deep cover.

I was working at a military base recently and someone there mentioned that a book they were using in a class was great. "Major ABC wrote that," said someone else. It was clear the men and women held this Major in high regard. Learning he was the author of a technical book they liked made them even more impressed.

If a career military man can use some of these techniques, you almost certainly can. Some creativity might be required, but we all tend to be creative in this field. This career military man actually seemed to be a Rock Star, or at least well on the path. Once he's retired from active duty it's a good bet he'll have plenty of choices for fun and rewarding work.

Why Would Anyone Care or Listen to Me?

We all have self-doubts at times, and the "Why would anyone listen to me?" syndrome is rampant, but dead wrong.

If your ideas are coherent and reasonably well articulated, people will listen. Some will definitely care. Your ideas do not need to be brilliant. Some may find them brilliant, but that doesn't matter.

Yes, some people won't listen to you, and that's ok – screw them. A lot of people, the most intelligent people, get their information, insights, and information from a wide variety of sources. And many will listen to you.

I learn a lot and get a lot of insights from people with far less experience, including my kids.

Even a newbie has something they can share.

Ethics – *Your* Comfort Level

Many of us are not comfortable promoting ourselves, and whether we use the word *promoting* or not, that is what we are talking about. Promotional tactics can easily be in the ethical gray zone, if not well into the red zone.

For example, I could describe myself as an "Award Winning, Amazon #1 Bestselling Author." It is true; however I was #1 in Amazon in an obscure category and the award is for my friend Dan Janal's "Cool Book of the Day Award." I do not describe myself as an award winning, Amazon #1 Bestselling author because although it's technically true, I find it to be misleading, sleazy, and yes, unethical.

However, just because a tactic is uncomfortable, does not mean it is in the gray zone. Worse, it could just be that many of us are simply not accustomed to and not comfortable with promoting ourselves.

Hint: Pushing your comfort level is absolutely fine at times.

Much of this is Mindset

Which of the following sounds better? Both are true.

▶ "I taught a bunch of technical people basic management principles and common sense."

▶ "I led a Leadership Bootcamp for the Navy."

These two statements carry very different impacts. There are no ethical issues here. Both are absolutely true and there is no deception. Obviously, I'd say "I led a Leadership Bootcamp for the Navy," and I did.

The "Home Online" Concept

You should have a home online, somewhere people can go to find out more about you, someplace you can point to from your email signature, profiles, and other places.

It may be obvious what your home online is or should be, or it may not. It could even be a company website, perhaps your bio on your company website, or it could be far more personal.

For example, when I was doing work with The Institute for Advanced Professional Studies, I could have used their one-page bio of me as my home online, or now I could use my one-page bio on *sans.org*. Right now I use one of my security oriented Websites, *InfosecRockStar.com*.

If you have no other home online, your LinkedIn profile makes a fine home online.

Testimonials

You can't say you're great. It's not believable and you'll come off as a pompous ass. However other people can say you're great and other positive things about you, and we typically call these statements testimonials. They may also be referred to as recommendations, comments, feedback, and more. Testimonials simply work extremely well to position you well, and many companies and individuals use them.

Results-oriented testimonials are best, but use what you can. For example, "Ted was great," is nice, but the results-oriented, "Ted taught me things I can use immediately," or "Ted fixed our horribly derailed SIEM deployment and amazingly brought the project to a close on time and under budget," are much better.

Here are a few actual testimonials I've used.

▶ *United Press International* calls Ted an "IT expert."

This one is not results oriented, and I would rather UPI called me an "Infosec Expert" or "Cyber Defense Guru," but "IT expert" is very nice too. UPI referred to me as an "IT expert" in a newspaper article, and we will talk a little bit about getting press coverage later.

▶ "Ted, to those about to rock, I salute you. Great videos and always enjoy listening and learning from you. I always pickup new tips and tricks." – Dr. Eric Cole

Dr. Eric Cole is a personal friend, but that doesn't make his testimonial less valuable or sincere. Eric is simply far better known in our field than I am, and his statements essentially bring me up to his level in the eyes of his many fans.

▶ "I am immensely proud to have you as a mentor, and as a friend." – Pierre Noel, Chief Information Security & Privacy Officer, Huawei

This testimonial is from a bigwig at Huawei and someone I've known and worked with for decades. I'm impressed by Pierre Noel as are many others, and he says impressive things about me. Many people have seen this testimonial and commented positively on it.

You may be able to use testimonials in many places, such as your website, in an email signature, on LinkedIn, or even in a CV or resume.

So how do you get testimonials? Some may just seemingly magically appear. I've gotten some great testimonials from traditional media, on LinkedIn, and in blog post and video comments.

You can also ask for testimonials. We won't go into this much, but LinkedIn allows you to easily ask, referring to them as recommendations. If you have a blog or do any video you can ask for them, usually as comments. All of my training clients have specifically requested them on feedback and evaluation forms, and I have used some of these. When you write a book it is common to send a draft to people asking for testimonials.

One last thing. When in doubt, ask if you can use a testimonial. People who gave them privately may not want them made public. Respect their wishes.

Some Easy Techniques for Letting the World Know you Rock

We are going to list some easy techniques to let the world know you rock. We will go over LinkedIn, reviews on Amazon, Facebook pages, leaving targeting comments on industry blogs, email signatures, simple one-page websites, and video. Yes, I am listing video as easy! Of course any of these techniques can be made more complex.

There are plenty of other potentially easy techniques, and we have not attempted to list everything possible here.

LinkedIn

LinkedIn is a professional social network. If you are not familiar with it, and most people are, it is not remotely like most other social media such as Facebook or Twitter. The emphasis is much more on professional than social.

LinkedIn is important because search engines love it, and also because it is widely used. For example, there is a lot of information online about me, yet my LinkedIn profile still comes up third in a Google search as of this writing.

It is debatable, but I believe all professionals should be on LinkedIn. Certainly the vast majority should.

Your LinkedIn profile is essentially an online CV or resume. There are many other features as well you can use or ignore. There are both free and paid versions. The free version is fine and most popular. Even Jason Alba, who wrote the first book on LinkedIn, uses the free version.

Reviews on Amazon

Amazon allows you to set up a profile, somewhat like LinkedIn, and review items. I suggest you consider reviewing professional books and other items. Be careful what you review. No off color items, please. The search engines also love to index Amazon profiles and reviews. If not much shows up about you in an online search, this is a good way to get some content up quickly.

Facebook Pages

Another idea is creating a Facebook Page for yourself. This is not a personal account/profile, but linked to your personal account. For example, I have a Facebook page many of you have "liked" called *Infosec Rock Star*. I could have used my own name for the Facebook page just as well. Quoting Facebook, "Pages are for businesses, brands, and organizations to share their stories and connect with people. Like profiles, you can customize Pages by posting stories, hosting events, adding apps and more. People who like your Page and their friends can get updates in News Feed."[10]

A Facebook page alone won't make you an Expert, but can help with visibility. It's a good place for you to post articles you have written and placed elsewhere, extending their reach.

Targeted Comments on Blogs

There are lots of great security blogs and most allow comments. Most comments allow a link from your name (remember the section on your name?). Link back to your home online: LinkedIn profile, website, etc.

There is no need to overthink this. You can just go leave some intelligent comments, something more than just, *me too*.

Comments help in several ways. On a popular blog, regular comments can and will increase your online visibility. Also, search engines often index your comments so they show up when people Google you. I have still comments from over a decade ago on Bruce Schneier's blog indexed and visible in Google.

The links back to your home online are valuable too. While a few people may follow them, equally important is that search engines will find and follow them and make it more likely your home online shows up high in the search engine results. Essentially search engines consider each link to be a vote of confidence that what is being linked to is valuable. This is sometimes called SEO (Search Engine Optimization) and is itself a horrifically complex and rapidly changing topic, although the basics are simple: good stuff online with links to it!

---

10   *Facebook.* Web. 20 Dec. 2016.

Email Signatures

Email is incredibly powerful. Entire companies, including security companies, have been built on mail. If you were born somewhere around 1986 or earlier, you may think email is an older technology, something you use to communicate with your parents and boss. You're wrong! Email is an incredible promotional and communication tool that is not going away any time soon.

There is a lot to email and we are just mentioning email signatures below.

Use an email signature. Link to your home(s) online and include anything else pertinent, perhaps an upcoming conference you'll be speaking at or an online article you've written. Make sure you test any links to make sure they work.

Here are a few examples of email signatures. The first one is from my friend Doc.

Doc Blackburn, CISSP
GSEC, GSLC, ITIL, GPEN, GCPM, PCI ISA, GISF,
HCISPP, GCIA
LinkedIn Profile
Do I Have Your Attention Now?
Text or Call: (720) 555-5555

I like how Doc has listed the most important certification with his name, and the others on the next line. "LinkedIn Profile" links to his LinkedIn profile. "Do I Have Your Attention Now" is the name of his blog and links to it.

Often when Doc has an upcoming speaking engagement, his email signature will include details and a link to the event as well.

Here is my current one.

Ted Demopoulos, Demopoulos Associates, Cyber Defense
The Infosec Rock Star Project:
Infosec Rock Star - Geek will only get you so far

It is pretty short and basic, says what I do, and links to the Infosec Rock Star project website, which is what I'm working primarily on today.

One of the bonuses

http://infosecrockstar.com/bonuses/ goes into using email effectively to build your image and fans.

The "One Page" Website

A simple, one-page website with your own domain name is very powerful and is an option for your home online. You have complete control, unlike sites such as Facebook, LinkedIn, and others. You have the option of extending it in the future should you desire. It satisfies the "you're expected to have a Website" criteria if applicable, and is just like an online brochure to showcase who you are.

There are places you can host a single page for free and they are okay, although they come and go and you do not have full control.

At one point I had a single page website at *teddemop.com*. It's no longer active, but was highly visible and did help get me work while it was active.

Video

Video can be very easy or very complex. Simple videos, shot with a smart phone, can be very powerful. Most phones produce high quality video today. They can be uploaded to video sharing sites such as YouTube, and search engines rank videos quite highly so they show up when people search on your name.

Some people immediately rebel when they hear video because they don't want to be videoed; however, simple screen capture is popular and works well too. Screen capture could show you demonstrating a tool or technique online or display PowerPoint or similar slides as you speak.

Of course you can also go wild with expensive equipment, fancy video effects, private hosting, and more, but that's not always necessary. It's ok to start small.

Some More Involved Techniques for Letting the World Know you Rock

Some more involved techniques include volunteering, podcasting, getting press coverage, doing surveys, speaking and writing, including articles, books, blogs, and more.

We will not cover these all in detail, and they will not all be applicable to everyone either. Just think of these as ideas.

Volunteering

Although volunteering at the local soup kitchen or Special Olympics as I just did is wonderful, that is not what I'm talking about. There are plenty of opportunities to volunteer at some industry conferences, with local user groups, and more. You do not remotely need much experience in Infosec to volunteer. Volunteering increases your visibility and can give you extensive networking opportunities.

Organizations are always looking for volunteers. Some examples include Stephanie Vanroelen volunteering for Brucon and Hak4Kidz, Larry Vandenaweele volunteering for Bsides Las Vegas and Brucon, and Thomas Hart who started volunteering with Bsides Boston, and now also volunteers with HOPE (Hackers On Planet Earth), ISACA New England, ISC2 Eastern Massachusetts, and more.

Getting involved with your local and not so local Infosec Community can be amazingly powerful. I know that at least of couple of you here have actually leveraged this to move into this field professionally and full time. The connections and friends you meet can be invaluable, and both what you learn and the visibility you generate are valuable as well. And you'll probably have fun too.

Podcasting

A Podcast is simply an audio or video blog. Think Internet radio or TV and you have the right idea. Podcasting can be a lot of work, and many consider it very rewarding. You might also have opportunities to be a guest on other people's podcasts.

Getting Press Coverage

Getting press coverage is a skill you can learn like anything else. We won't go into it in much detail here but cover some basics.

It doesn't matter if anyone sees the original media coverage. Being able to claim you were quoted or featured in various media carries a lot of weight.

I've been quoted or featured in hundreds of articles including in the *Wall Street Journal*, *CNN Money*, *Investor's Business Daily*, *USA Today*, *United Press International*, the *Chicago Tribune*, the *Los Angeles Times*, the *Boston Globe*, the *Boston Herald*, the *Sacramento Bee*, *CIO Today*, *Information Week*, and even *Pizza Marketplace News*. This doesn't mean I'm smart, but it impresses potential clients and employers for sure.

I've gotten much of this press coverage using an inexpensive service that connects reporters and Rock Stars like you called *PrLeads. com* and run by Dan Janal, who has become a personal friend. There is also the free but very competitive HARO, Help a Reporter Out, at *www.helpareporter.com.*

You can also pitch reporters directly, hire public relations professionals, and issue press releases.

Getting press is not rocket science. It does take time and work, however. There is a learning curve involved.

Surveys

A survey is a good way to get visibility, and you might even get paid to do it.

Here are three quick examples:

▶ I was paid to do a survey for a large security company at which I interviewed all their customer facing security people and reported back on their security knowledge and how to improve their security acumen.

▶ A large club I belonged to was considering a survey of their members and I volunteered to help. The members included lots of influential people in high tech.

▶ I also took initiative and did a short survey on phishing awareness when phishing was relatively new.

You could just pick a topic and do a survey, like I did on phishing awareness. Afterward, I issued a simple press release and posted it on my website, my blog, and Twitter.

Speaking

A Speaker is an Expert

If you are The Speaker you are automatically considered an Expert, and speakers get a lot of visibility. Not just when speaking, but depending on the speech, from pre- and post-speech promotion and visibility.

Many Rock Stars speak, whether it's in front of crowds of thousands or three people; sometimes live or on video or audio podcasts or other media.

Some of you will immediately revolt here, as you claim you do not know enough yet to speak and are perhaps terrified of speaking. Keep in mind, we all have useful information we can share. Maybe you only have one year in Infosec, but is there a case study from work of interest that you can share? If not the details, perhaps just lessons learned?

Or maybe you have researched something you are interested in, and can talk for a few minutes. Maybe even something like home router security or home security systems or cameras. It can be anything you're familiar with; it doesn't need to be from your work.

No one is asking you to speak for five or six days as I often do, just to get up for a few minutes and speak. As a professional, you *will* occasionally need to give presentations or speak, so why not become good at it? It pays enormous dividends and isn't difficult.

You Get Better at Speaking by Speaking

You get better at speaking by speaking, and there are plenty of opportunities as organizations are always looking for speakers.

You can even gain experience with organizations like the highly regarded Toastmasters, a non-profit club that exists to help people "improve their communication, public speaking, and leadership skills."[11] Many of my students and friends have joined Toastmasters to develop and improve their speaking skills. It is dirt cheap, and even

---

11   "Toastmasters International." *Wikipedia*. Wikimedia Foundation, Web. 20 Dec. 2016.

in semi-rural New Hampshire there are twelve clubs within twenty-five miles of me.

Maybe you are afraid to speak on Infosec to Infosec people because you don't have much experience. Keep in mind that interest in security among laypeople runs super high today with all the ongoing hacks and news coverage. Looking just at the Rotary International Club, there are eleven chapters within twenty-five miles of me and they each need a speaker every week for over six hundred speakers a year. I'll bet if I contacted them all, which might take thirty minutes, and offered a talk on protecting yourself or your children online, several would be interested and would maybe even buy me lunch or dinner.

If you are too apprehensive to speak on security or want some more support, speak on something else to build your skills. I've spoken on ham radio, blogging, fly fishing, marketing, and Champagne. No doubt you have other interests you can speak about. If you can't find a ready audience, and various groups and clubs are always looking for speakers, you can podcast or be a guest on a podcast or do a YouTube video on anything you are interested in – even anonymously. I have an informative "Fly Fishing for Striped Bass" YouTube video with just me speaking on camera that has over sixteen thousand views, despite low production quality. It gave me experience and people love it. Besides live video, simple screen capture video works well, whether of the screen as you are demonstrating something, maybe a hacker tool, or simple presentation slides as you speak.

Better Speaking Gigs

Speaking at service clubs and churches and the boy scouts and community centers will get you lots of experience speaking and some local expert status, and is just a beginning, although you do not need to start here if you are somewhat comfortable speaking to groups. There are lots of conferences and local user groups that always need speakers. You probably cannot start at Black Hat or RSA or ShmooCon, but you may be able to speak at BSides (and they have specific Security BSides too), other smaller conferences, and local user groups.

The more you speak, the more you get asked to speak.

You can even get paid to speak, but don't make that a goal, at least initially. I often speak for free, although most of my talks are paid. Kevin Mitnick reportedly gets $25,000 a speech. Sir Richard Branson, Lance Armstrong, Al Gore, and others make $100,000 per speech and more.

Let's not get ahead of ourselves. There is speaking to help build and cement Expert to Rock Star Status, and speaking for big bucks because you are already a Rock Star and great speaker—two very different things, although there is certainly some overlap.

Some Quick Speaking Tips

Most audiences want to like you, so relax. Yes, occasionally there are hostile audiences, but they are rare, and you are unlikely to encounter them.

Make sure your talk is logically organized with a beginning, body, and ending.

You can and often should do a dry run or more of your talk. I usually stand up and go through my talk out loud.

If you are using slides, don't just read the slides. Use the bullet points and pictures instead as cues to reinforce what you are saying.

Make eye contact with members of the audience and smile. Of course, with a big group you can only make eye contact with the few up front, but that is fine.

Vary your voice. Not only do you not want to speak in a monotone voice, but you also don't want to do your whole talk in a fast, loud, and excited voice. Varying your voice is key.

Use stories to illustrate points. They work, and are far more interesting than just facts. They help keep interest and more.

Engage the audience, which is sometimes hard. You can ask for questions or feedback at any time, and if you don't get any responses say something like, "Good, seems you are all following this," or "A common question here is . . ."

We could talk about speaking for days. These are just a few quick tips.

Writing

An author, just like a speaker, is automatically perceived as an Expert and beyond and authors can get a lot of visibility. Writing is a professional skill well worth mastering.

A Book

You *can* write a book. It's easier than you think.

A traditional book does incredible wonders to create instant Expert status and beyond. Ideally, this happens with a traditional publisher, but self-publishing has no negative stigma today. A Kindle book is much easier to create and can be much shorter as well, and it gives automatic publishing credibility. Another option is simply an e-book released online, maybe free or in exchange for an email address.

You can even slap an ISBN number on your ebook (or anything else you write). Keep in mind that a book is merely an information product. Other examples of information products include video, audio, and hybrid products. There can be lots of money and visibility in these.

Besides books, there are many other things you can "author" and use to position yourself as an author, including blogs, whitepapers, case studies, and polls.

A Blog

Blogs are great but can be a lot of work, although they don't have to be.

You write a blog in a conversational tone, no formal language or grammar necessary, and update it maybe once or twice a month or more.

I have written two of the first books ever on blogging (which does make me an Expert, but don't read my books as they are out of date). My viewpoint on blogging has changed. The suggestion was once to blog frequently, at least once a week, preferably several times a week. Sure, that works, but blogging once or twice a month is sufficient to help build Expert status these days. Blogging once a month is not a lot of work.

Consider starting a temporary or "throw away" blog to get some experience blogging and see if you want to continue and/or to simply practice writing and become better at it. For example, this could be something leading up to a one-time event, and can even be anonymous. Obviously an anonymous blog won't give you visibility, but you can practice and hopefully improve your writing and see if you enjoy blogging.

You also may be able to write guest posts for other people's blogs. That is far less work.

Some Other Writing Options

An email newsletter works well. Get people to sign up by offering something free to download, and also post to your blog or website or any of your social media accounts. I like AWeber for handling email addresses and sending bulk email. Don't worry if almost no one subscribes at first; that list will grow over time. Regularly producing an email newsletter will also help make you a better writer, and as I said before, writing is a critical professional skill.

A useful list of resources on any one particular topic can be very valuable. The length doesn't matter; it can be only one page. Sometimes shorter is better anyway. I'm currently looking into creating a resource list of writing and speaking information to help others.

A case study. People love case studies, and even if you have almost no experience, no doubt you've done something and learned from your successes and failures, and what you've learned *will* be useful to others.

You could document some useful process or procedure. At one company I spent a lot of time consulting with, we occasionally had to change the IP addresses of certain machines. Usually it was simple, but occasionally there were glitches with some of the application software. One young employee spent a very few hours and figured out all the interactions, then wrote up a simple tested procedure that always worked. Any of the technical people he worked with could have done this, but only he did it. It absolutely elevated his status within the organization. As time went on, he documented another two "how to" procedures and was absolutely considered an uber geek and Expert in the group, even though any decent technical person could have written these. He took the initiative and rightly received a lot of credit and elevated status.

Mind maps are another thought. Many people love mind maps, whether they are on pen testing, forensics, or email marketing.

Tweeting will not position you as an Expert alone; however, like a Facebook page you can use it to extend the reach of things you have previously written.

Did you know you even LinkedIn has allowed people to post articles for over a year and millions have been posted? I've never written anything specifically for LinkedIn, but have reused and sometimes slightly adapted articles from *InfosecRockstar.com* and other sources. People absolutely do see and read them.

This is not an exclusive list at all, but I hope these suggestions are helpful. You will likely encounter other opportunities as you move forward.

Side Note on Intellectual Property

As we are generating value and making that value visible, we are more and more likely to be generating intellectual property. Intellectual property is protected by law just like physical property is, although laws do vary depending on jurisdiction. The four types of intellectual property generally protected by law are listed below. Quotes are from the United States Patent and Trademark Office.

▶ Copyrights – "protection provided to the authors of 'original works of authorship' including literary, dramatic, musical, artistic, and certain other intellectual works, both published and unpublished"

▶ Patents – "the grant of a property right to the inventor" for a something which is novel, non-obvious, and has utility

▶ Trademarks/Servicemarks – "a word, name, symbol, or device that is used in trade with goods to indicate the source of the goods and to distinguish them from the goods of others"

▶ Trade Secrets – anything non-public that helps you compete. Could be a how you stock the shelves, how you hire, how you decide which projects to go forward with, etc.

I will mention again that I have no legal training and this cannot be taken as legal advice; consult counsel if needed.

We will concentrate on copyright here. Any recorded form of expression (for example a podcast, an article on LinkedIn, a blog, a letter to your mother, almost anything) is copyrighted by default. The word *Copyright* and the Copyright symbol © are often applied to copyrighted works to avoid innocent infringement, but have no legal meaning. You can also formally file for a Copyright to give you additional legal protections.

What this means is that you hold legal copyright to most things you create, whether written, recorded audio, video, and more. Many of you will be and probably already are generating valuable Intellectual Property. Intellectual Property can be reused, sold, licensed, and more. You are generating valuable, including in a financial sense, assets.

A Possible IP Opportunity

Releasing or lessening your intellectual property rights can allow your IP and the value it has to spread further, while spreading your name and expertise. Sometimes this can make sense.

For example, Creative Commons (*CreativeCommons.org*), has six licenses you can choose from, which, in their words, provide "free, easy-to-use copyright licenses providing a simple, standardized way to give you permission to share and use your creative work— on conditions of your choice."[12] I once wrote an e-book and applied a Creative Commons license to it, allowing it to freely spread with the restriction that it not be modified, loosening my default copyright rights significantly. More than forty thousand copies were downloaded, and it absolutely resulted in follow-on consulting work. It would not have spread as far if I hadn't relaxed my copyright restrictions.

This book was preceded and is based on feedback from a previous a sixty-page *Infosec Rockstar* PDF, which was copyrighted and required an email address to download. If I had relaxed the copyright,

---

12   @creativecommons. "When we share, everyone wins - Creative Commons." Creative Commons. Accessed December 20, 2016. https://creativecommons. org/.

allowing sharing, removed the email address requirement, and let it spread freely, there is no there is no doubt far more people would have downloaded it and it would have spread further. I didn't, as the restrictions facilitated getting feedback, but still may in the future.

Software with intellectual property restrictions removed, commonly called Open Source, is another opportunity. It has certainly given some people Rock Star Status, such as Linus Torvalds, Fyodor of Nmap fame, and many more.

Action Step: List a few ideas you are going to pursue to let the world know you rock.

For example, create or update a LinkedIn profile, consider a one-page website, or review a few books on Amazon.

Make a short list of ideas and take action!

4
OWN YOUR FANS

• • • • • • •

The Fan Concept

A fan is an enthusiastic devotee, an ardent admirer. The term is commonly used to refer to fans of bands, sports teams, and entertainers, but has much wider applicability.

Your fans are people who think you rock, who are enthusiastic about what you do, and who admire your work and results.

You add value to your fans. That is why they are fans. Maybe they love your music, or your cooking, or you make compliance with regulations as painless as possible. Now, just because you add value to someone's life doesn't mean they are necessarily going to be a fan. Some people just aren't going to like you much or at all, no matter what. That's ok; it's normal. Just get used to it and don't worry about it. Continue to add value.

Fans can be and often are mutual. Fans are interconnected. You can be a fan of someone who is also your fan. In some areas you may lead them, while in others areas they may lead you.

For example, when it comes to exercise and fitness, I listen to Dr. Eric Cole. When it comes to food and drink, Eric listens to me. When it comes to Infosec, there is a lot of mutual cooperation.

Note: Life isn't a Popularity Contest

Fans are great, but life isn't a popularity contest.

If you're not upsetting someone, you probably aren't doing much of significance. There is an old saying, "If you're not pissing someone off, you probably aren't doing anything important."

Now please don't misunderstand me, I don't want to upset anyone and you shouldn't either. But I do upset people sometimes and you are going to. Sometimes doing your job well upsets people. Continue to do your job well.

Johnny Rotten takes it a step further when he says, "If you are pissing people off, you know you are doing something right," and depending on your role that may actually sometimes be right. I've had roles in which I was hired as a disruptive influence; I was hired to change things, but most people love the status quo and hate change.

More on Mutual Fans

Great business and personal relationships are win-win. Both sides add value to each other. It doesn't matter what specifically that value is.

In the same way you don't need to analyze why you like certain music or hobbies, you don't need to analyze or justify why you're a fan of someone in the industry. I happen to like broccoli, jazz, and the Grateful Dead. As a geek, I could analyze why, but it doesn't matter.

I just like them. They add value to my life. I could say I'm fans of them, although I usually reserve the term for people.

You have a lot of relationships, both business and personal, in which you add value to each other's lives. On the previous page I said, "You add value to your fans." It's common to be mutual fans: for two people to be fans of each other because they add something to each other's life. My first boss right out of school, Randy Barron, is someone I'm a big fan of and I'm going to claim he's a fan of mine. We pretty quickly became friends, and are still very much in touch; I'm seeing him later this week, actually. Not only did he hire me, but I returned the favor and hired him a few years later. I'd work for him again in a second, even though the last thing I want is a boss. I might even hire him, although I don't want people reporting directly to me right now.

Hopefully your boss is a fan or yours and vice-versa. This is ideal.

I'm an enormous fan of many people I work with. I know quite a few of you personally, and I'm a massive fan of several of you. Many of you are doing amazing things that I know of, whether or not you think you are doing amazing things. Many of you have added and are adding value to my life, and I'm excited and happy to know you. In some cases, just knowing you and what you're doing is an inspiration, and that's great. I know you are all being very proactive, because you're reading this, and being proactive is impressive in itself. Most people aren't that way.

Be Your Own Fan (You'd Better)

If you are not a fan of yourself, why should anyone else be? If you don't follow yourself, why should anyone else? Self-confidence is essential.

It is normal for humans to have self-doubts; we all do. However, confidence is essential to being a Rock Star. You certainly do not want to have an inflated ego, an excessive sense of self-importance, or any similar attitude. In general, I believe we do pretty well here in Infosec: we have lots of Rock Stars but few enormous egos.

It is exceedingly common for people (including your closest friends and fans) to try to talk you out of your best ideas. Most people, including the dearest of friends, like the status quo and resist change. Great ideas tend to be disruptive. You need self-confidence to go forward with your ideas.

When I left my last full-time job many years ago at Hewlett-Packard to be an independent consultant, I got enormous pushback from friends and family. The economy was bad, I had a seemingly great job, I didn't have any business experience (and as a consultant you *are* running a business). There are *always* reasons not to do something. That doesn't mean you shouldn't do that something.

Now, certainly working for yourself is not ideal for everyone, but it has worked out spectacularly well for me. Yes, of course I had self-doubts, and they were amplified by well-meaning friends and family, but I knew I had to do it, or at very least give it a substantial try.

I had enough self-confidence to move forward. I was enough of a fan of myself that I pushed myself to the next big thing.

I also had a lot of people convinced that I would be wasting my time, or possibly even worse, harming my career, following this Infosec Rock Star idea. Although my first few talks were successful, some friends and colleagues gently, and sometimes not so gently, tried to tell me I shouldn't pursue this any further. When I put up the *InfosecRockStar.com* website, feedback was extremely positive, yet some of my closest friends and colleagues tried to dissuade me. Ditto for when I wrote my first short e-book that morphed into this tome, and when I started teaching my successful Infosec Rock Star courses.

Of course I had some doubts; that is simply human nature. But I had enough self-confidence to press forward, even although at times things did not remotely go as planned. A lot of times things went sideways, meaning I was making no significant progress. I didn't let that dissuade me.

Another example is the first *Chicken Soup for the Soul* book written by Jack Canfield and Mark Victor Hansen. Their book was rejected by dozens of publishers before finally being accepted by a small publisher, and is now a franchise with over 250 books, dog food, and more. They needed to be fans of themselves and their work to push on to eventual success through the dozens of rejections. I'm sure well-meaning friends encouraged them to stop banging their heads on this seemingly failure of an idea, which eventually became a massive success.

Humans are Not Perfect: Fans Included

Certainly we are all human and humans are not perfect. For example, Tony, who does occasional gardening work for me, is a phenomenal human being and a spectacular gardener. I am a fan of his. My ex-wife once hired him to work on her vintage VW Bug. However, it didn't work out as expected. VW Bug work is not his forte.

We also all have limitations and imperfections. Some we simply need to know. In my case, I know I have no business reverse engineering malware professionally (although I may experiment with it at times) or working in finance. Similarly, the once every ten years or so when I show up at the wrong airport, my clients just laugh, even though it may cause a temporary inconvenience. At least they did last time. And when I landed in San Diego during Comic-Con, perhaps the world's biggest convention, and found I had no hotel reservations at 1:00 a.m. due to cascading failures, I just laughed. I did eventually find an overpriced (and very smelly) hotel room. When I landed in Saudi Arabia for the first time ever, and at 2:00 a.m. I had no promised driver at the small and remote airport, I didn't get upset. No one, including my clients, is perfect. In all three cases we simply worked to improve our processes, knowing they would never be one-hundred-percent perfect. Nothing and no one is one-hundred-percent perfect. Nothing and no one is "all purpose."

Our fans ideally will smile at our limitations/imperfections, just like Deadheads would smile when Jerry Garcia forgot song lyrics.

Although friends often try to talk people out of their best ideas, at least equally often, we have to try to convince people, including our fans, to do what is in their best interest. Sometimes we may be convincing them that we are doing the right thing, taking the best course of action. That is where negotiating (although we often use different terms), understanding how influence works, and leadership (all somewhat interrelated) come into play.

Changing the Default

For whatever reason, sometimes we want to change other people's actions or thinking or behavior. This might be social engineering our boss for the greater good, getting members of our team to adopt a specific approach, negotiating a lower price on a car, leading our fans in a specific and hopefully mutually beneficial direction, and more.

Sometimes we simply cannot change the default to what we want it to be, and we must accept it. For example, if you are trying to change your friend's political views via Facebook posts, it's probably not going to work.

Let's discuss negotiations, both informal and formal, then the scientific principles of how influence works, and also leadership, both traditional and non-traditional (the Internet has changed leadership opportunities a lot). You may or may not be the boss, but people follow your lead because they are your fans.

Negotiations, Formal and Informal

We negotiate a lot, whether we use that term of not. We do it in everyday life, including both professionally and personally. Hey, I was just negotiating with old friends over where we were going to meet. Although no one was thinking of the terms *negotiate* or *negotiating* or *negotiations*, that is exactly what was going on.

Sometimes We Need to Negotiate

As you move toward Rock Star, negotiation skills increase in importance. These are both formal and very often informal negotiations. As we said, commonly we won't even use the word *negotiate* or *negotiations*. "What shall we do for dinner?" and, "When will the report be ready?" are both preludes to informal negotiations.

In the western world, few people have much experience with formal negotiations, usually just for buying houses and cars. In much of the world people negotiate for nearly everything, including the price of a loaf of bread, a scarf, shoes, essential everyday items.

Some people are formally trained as negotiators. I'm not, and I'm going to assume you are not either, but knowing the basics of negotiations can go a long way.

In the Bazaar, Muscat, Oman, with my friend Roxy

Roxy: "I *love* that scarf. It's absolutely gorgeous! How much is it?"

Me, nearly interrupting: "It's a nice scarf, but the colors aren't ideal for you."

Roxy: "No, it's perrrrrrfect!"

Do you think Roxy got a good deal?

As in most bazaars, at least every one I've been to, there are no fixed prices. Everything involves negotiations, or bargaining, if you prefer that term.

Most of us, whether we bargain at all or not, can quickly tell that Roxy did not get a good deal on the scarf. She made it blatantly obvious that she loved it and was probably going to buy it regardless of the price. I tried to counter and help by commenting that the colors were not perfect for her. Perhaps falsely; I know nothing about women's scarves.

The proprietor of this store had little reason to offer her a good price, and he didn't. Roxy wasn't a hundred percent clueless (maybe only 99 percent), and insisted on bargaining once the proprietor had quoted a price. He came down a little since that's how the game is played, but not very much. He didn't have to. She had an incredibly weak bargaining position, having already played her hand—having made her feelings and intentions obvious.

By the way, this little store and the proprietor were great. Count me as a fan. I did go back and buy some scarves from him the next day. I got a better deal than Roxy!

Distributive Negotiations

In Distributive Negotiations, there is a "fixed pie," or fixed value. The more I get, the less you get. The less I get, the more you get. It's a win-lose scenario.

The negotiations above were distributive. The more Roxy paid for the scarf, the more money the proprietor got and the less she had left. The less she paid for the scarf, the more money she had left and the less the proprietor had.

It's similar if you are buying a car, or a security appliance, or any simple transaction; the more you pay, the less money you have left.

However not all negotiations are distributive, or win-lose, and a common negotiation mistake is assuming they are.

In Marmaris, Turkey

This is a true story, although to some Westerners it seems hard to believe. I had gone out to dinner with a few people I met while traveling in Marmaris, Turkey. The restaurant was highly recommended, and did not serve alcohol, which was fine. Several of us wanted a beer afterward and the owner sent us to a nearby bar.

I went first to scout out the bar.

Me: "I'll take a beer; how much?"

Bartender: "Ten Lira."

Me: "I have ten friends coming soon. If the price is better, we will stay and have a few."

Negotiations ensued.

Bartender: "Also, I'll throw in a free shot of tequila for everyone."

Me: "Deal!"

The bar was quite empty, as it was both early in the evening and offseason. I asked what a beer cost, making it clear I would have one, but if the price was good I had a flock of friends across the road at the restaurant who would definitely have at least a beer or two. As the bar was pretty empty, I had a lot of value to offer, a bunch of people to buy drinks, as well as make the bar seem lively and more likely that other people would stop by.

We negotiated; the price of beer was reduced 50 percent, quite substantially. The owner wouldn't go any lower it appeared.

Suddenly he added a shot of tequila for everyone, sweetening the pot. That added substantial value to us and a very low cost to him, as he had a bottle of tequila that apparently had been sitting on the shelf unused for a very long time.

Integrative Negotiations

In Integrative Negotiations, both sides work together to increase value. The bar scenario was an example of an Integrative Negotiation.

I fairly quickly increased value by added my ten beer-drinking friends. The bartender added value by adding tequila. My friends cost me nothing. The tequila cost the bartender very little.

As another example, if you are buying software, you may be able to get training bundled in your negotiations. Training often has a very high value to you, but to the vendor it might merely consist of printing a few more books and adding a few seats to a room.

Distributive vs. Integrative Negotiations

Don't assume a negotiation is one or the other. Things can change and real-world negotiations often combine both approaches and can change back and forth.

Often negotiations with fans are integrative. For example, last night, my son and I (and I'd like to think we are mutual fans of each other despite his occasionally being an impetuous teenager and me occasionally being a grumpy old man) were talking about dinner and he really wanted to go to his favorite Mexican restaurant. I agreed if he would help me walk the dog and fix the electronic dog fence first.

Another example happened with a client. I had an initiative I wanted to undertake on his behalf, and was met with lukewarm enthusiasm at best. I was certain it would add significant value, but he was not. In our discussions (and we never used the word "negotiations") we agreed that I would undertake the project but we had some modifications, notably bundling a smaller related project he championed into the whole.

Attempt to Build Mutual Trust

Attempt to build mutual trust with whomever you are (formally or informally) negotiating with. If there already is some relationship in place, perhaps you already are fans of each other, there may be a significant level of mutual trust as well. You may also have mutual goals, often the case professionally, which can help. If not, try to build mutual trust.

There will be times some people are not entirely truthful and may outright lie in negotiations. This can be ethical and unethical at times. We could debate whether omitting facts is dishonest; often times it absolutely is not. For example, if you need to get/buy/build/procure whatever it is you are negotiating about quickly, you do not need to disclose your timetable. If you have a specific budget, you do not need to make it known.

I went back to the shop where Roxy had bought her scarf the next day. The proprietor had quality scarves and seemed to know quite a bit about them. I looked at lots of scarves, dodging questions on what I exactly was looking for. I wanted to buy several scarves for both myself and as gifts, but I did not disclose that information. He had some great advice on scarves and especially the styles and colors that would work for me. I picked one I liked and began negotiating. We came to a price. I mentioned I might want more than one. We started talking about three in particular. The per-scarf price changed. I ended up with three scarves for myself and three children's scarves for a little less than the original price of two of the scarves. I also got him to throw in a small child's purse at the end.

Did we build mutual trust? Some, absolutely. He trusted I was serious about buying scarves and was negotiating in good faith. I trusted and took his advice on styles and colors, and perhaps my favorite scarf is now one I never initially considered at first but he persuaded me to buy; after all, he is the scarf expert.

Knowledge is Power

In any negotiation, knowledge is power. The more you know, the better. Professional negotiators do enormous research before entering into negotiation sessions. They may know more about your organization, your products or services, your fixed costs, and variable costs and more than you do.

Specifically, Roxy had little idea of the value of similar scarves, which was not good for her. When I went back, I did.

In the case of the bar with my friends, I did know roughly the price of a beer, that it was offseason, and that the bar was obviously empty. This was good for me; it strengthened my bargaining position.

Last time I bought a new car, before even visiting a dealer, I did quite a bit of research into cars, and very specifically what dealer costs were for the ones I was considering. When I bought my house, I did research on similar houses that had been sold recently and what they cost.

Sometimes a lot of knowledge may not be practically available. Do what you can to not appear ignorant.

What if it Doesn't Work Out?

A good agreement is win-win—good for both sides. This isn't always possible, and some negotiations should be and will be abandoned.

We stated that knowledge is power in negotiations, and one prime piece of knowledge is what options you have should you fail to reach an agreement. The more options the better.

The concept of the Best Alternative To A Negotiated Agreement (BATNA) comes from Roger Fisher and William Ury in their 1981 bestselling book, *Getting to Yes: Negotiating Without Giving In*. What is your best alternative? Doing without? Going to another source? Building it/creating it yourself?

With Roxy and the scarf, she had clearly fallen in love with that scarf. Not getting the scarf would have been painful. She made it obvious that she didn't have an attractive BATNA; she wanted *that* scarf. That was a massive disadvantage for her. When I went back I knew there were plenty of other people selling scarves in the bazaar, and I also could have happily bought something else or nothing at all.

With the bar in Marmaris, although the bartender and I didn't discuss it, it was obvious there were plenty of other places to get a beer: other bars, stores, and of course we also could have not gotten a beer at all. These were all advantages to me.

You always want to have a good BATNA, or at least appear to have one, to strengthen your negotiating position.

No Emotions?

Professional negotiators may be trained to negotiate with zero emotions but we are humans so there will always be emotions. Your emotions are not your friend in negotiating, although some negotiators feign emotion or may attempt to arouse emotion in you to their advantage.

Roxy's clear cut emotion (she *loved* the scarf) did not help. Car dealers will commonly use emotion to sell cars. For example, if a man mentions he is going to check with his wife, car dealers will often challenge the man's masculinity.

"What, you're not allowed to make a decision without checking with your wife? A real man can make his own decisions, and you seem like a real man to me; aren't you?"

I am certainly not suggesting you ignore your emotions. Acknowledge your emotions and try to identify the trigger. What are your emotions and why are they there? Emotions exist for a reason, and they can at times absolutely be helpful in negotiations if you acknowledge and understand them. Arousing emotions in others can sometimes be helpful in negotiating. People often agree to things based on emotions and rationalize their decision afterward based on facts.

Anchoring

The party who states the first price has the advantage because that price acts as an anchor for decision making. It is especially important if you have no idea what something is worth or what the other person is thinking. For example, is a piece of art worth around $100 or $10,000? When I have no idea what something is worth, I usually get the other party to state the first price, even if they do not want to. Remember, knowledge is power, and by getting the other side to suggest a price first, you make them reveal some information.

Wikipedia describes anchoring as, "a cognitive bias that describes the common human tendency to rely too heavily on the first piece of information offered when making decisions."[13]

I am currently talking to a big IT consulting company with little security expertise about a retainer agreement. I neither know their definition of retainer, as it can vary significantly, nor what kind of monetary commitment they want. Do they want a certain number of hours per month, or simply access to my brain to ask occasional questions with any project work falling under a separate agreement? Are they thinking $2,000 per month or $5,000 per week? I'll let them propose something first. They may suggest something that works well for them that is also in my favor. And if they suggest something entirely unacceptable, such as my being ready to jump through hoops at a moment's notice for $10,000 a year, I can just say no.

Finding/Removing Authority

Who has the authority to authorize the deal? Is the actual business decision-maker in the room? These are important questions. Both sides commonly try to find who has the real authority.

I always make sure I am in negotiation with the person who is actually authorized to make the deal. Sometimes you will have lower

13   "Anchoring." *Wikipedia*. Wikimedia Foundation, Accessed December 20, 2016. https://en.wikipedia.org/wiki/Anchoring.

level people thrown at you first who can only say no, but who cannot say yes. We call these people gatekeepers. Questions like, "Whose budget does this come from?" and, "Who will be responsible for this agreement?" are useful.

As a consultant, I often insist that ethically I must talk to the person whose budget is paying for the project or service to get to the real decision-maker, the person who has the authority to authorize deals. Practically, I believe I almost always need to for any significant deal.

Conversely, you *can* remove authority from the room to your advantage. You could say something to the effect of, "To agree to something of this magnitude, I must consult my business partners," or, "My boss will kill me if I agree to this." I find this especially useful if someone is trying to pressure me in negotiations.

Speed Kills

Negotiations take time and often cannot be rushed. Ideally, you get to know and trust (at least a little) the other party. I've had negotiations in the Pacific Rim that didn't truly start for an entire year. The other party wanted to meet multiple times to get to know me before we even started to discuss any deal. Most situations don't take this long, but they can take quite a bit of time.

At one time, I was working in San Francisco and staying in a hotel for ten weeks along with most of my team. One night, I came back from having dinner at the restaurant across the street with a few co-workers. Every time I had gone to the restroom, it had been occupied, which was not a big problem, but by the time I got to my hotel room I really needed to use the bathroom. The landline phone rang as I entered the room so I answered it. Cell service was spotty, so a friend had figured out where I was staying and tracked me down. My friend Jim wanted me to agree on my rate for an upcoming work engagement in Hong Kong, which was interesting as I hadn't even agreed to go to Hong Kong yet.

"Jim, I gotta use the bathroom; give me two minutes," I said.

"Fine Ted, just say you'll come for $800 a day plus expenses, and you'll get to hang out in Hong Kong," replied Jim.

I had to use the bathroom. Jim insisted he had zero time to wait. I refused to lower my rate, which was well above $800 per day, and after less than two minutes of speed negotiations I got what I asked for with zero concessions. If Jim had waited maybe two to three minutes, I would have been happy to have negotiated, but apparently it was a check-list item he wanted handled immediately. I had my several hundred dollars a day more and an agreement of business class travel or better.

Do *not* let anyone rush you! Haste or over-eagerness to reach a deal results in mistakes. You can always say, "This is important and I need time to think this over," or something similar. I have been known to use expletives when the other side is trying to rush me.

Although you shouldn't let anyone rush you, they may have valid reasons for wanting to complete negotiations quickly and be willing to make concessions. Keep an open mind.

Once I was at a "no haggle" car dealership where car prices were fixed and they simply offered a fair price. Nothing was negotiable. Well, everything was negotiable as it always is. I arrived tired and a little before closing, so not the best time, but I was literally driving by while on my way home from a trip. There were three cars of the same type and any one would have done. I wanted to buy the car outright and sell the current car I was driving separately. I had done my homework, and knew the price they asked was very fair, and I also knew what my car was worth if I sold it independently.

I told the salesman, "I'm going to buy one of these cars, probably tomorrow. I need to think on the colors and also see them during the daytime." The salesman wanted to sell me the car immediately; they always do, as they know most people who leave a car dealership never return, despite what they may intend or say.

It was the last day of the month, and the salesman wanted credit for selling it that month. He dropped the "non-negotiable" price, added the protection package for free, and bought the car I was driving for more than I was going to try to sell it for. Forty-five minutes later, I was driving away in my new car; the dealership employees had emptied my old car and put my belongings in a box, plus handed me fifteen dollars in change they had found in my old car.

Always Make Sure any Contract You Sign has the Exact Details you Agreed On

Once, while negotiating intellectual property rights over a security course I had written, we immediately agreed upon a price of $18,000. Simple, right? It took five more weeks of negotiations to agree to terms, and another two weeks to agree to wording on the contract. In the end, I got what I wanted, $18,000, and the company I was negotiating with got non-exclusive intellectual property rights to the course with a restriction that they could not compete with me at my existing clients. I wouldn't have gotten that if I was in a hurry. And I wouldn't have had the details/wording in the contract right if I hadn't spent the extra two weeks.

Never Negotiate Against Yourself

People often negotiate against themselves. This is a common problem.

State your position and then shut up. It is the next person's turn to talk. Whether they speak in five seconds or five minutes, it is their turn. Silence can be wonderful. If they try to prompt you to say more, refuse; you are waiting for them. You can say, "It's your turn," or, "I'm waiting for your response," or something similar.

I was partnering with a colleague on a potential project. My partner, as we had agreed, said to the client, "We can do the project as discussed for $45,000." Then after a slight silence he interjected, "But if that's too expensive we can do it for less." He should have kept quiet while waiting for a response. This is a prime example of negotiating against yourself. I had a strong temptation to hit this person, and I'm quite non-violent.

Negotiating Summary

We are always negotiating. We make agreements and resolve conflicts with people all day long. Often we don't use the word *negotiate* or think of our discussions as negotiations, but they are.

There are both Distributive and Integrative Negotiations; often both are combined in the real world. Knowledge is power; negotiate slowly; don't become emotional.

As you move to Rock Star status, you are more likely to engage in formal negotiations, although knowledge of negotiation techniques are helpful for everyone, even in non-formal discussions, which can range from what you're doing for dinner to discussing what your highest value activities are with your boss.

Remember that the negotiation isn't over until it is over. Details you previously agreed on *can* be revisited. Everything is negotiable, even things that might not have originally seemed negotiable.

The Science of Influence

Yes, influence has been studied by scientists, and of course it is related to negotiations, but is broader in scope.

Talk to an Infosec person about influence and they usually think social engineering. It turns out influence, which certainly includes social engineering, has been studied by scientists for many years. A lot of what we consider to be effective social engineering is actually based on folklore and may or may not be very effective. Rock Stars are effective.

Influence is simply getting people to do what you want them to do. Obviously, getting people to do what you want is enormously helpful in being effective.

Influence, The Psychology of Persuasion by Dr. Robert B. Cialdini is the classic book on influence. It's a fast and easy read and highly recommended. The principles are applicable to business, your career, personal life, and just about anything else.

And there is nothing sleazy about it, although influence can be used for the good, the bad, and even the ugly.

Influence as described by Dr. Cialdini's book is based on six universal principles, and these principles are very useful in negotiations and leadership, among other things.

The Six Principles

The six principles are (Commitment and) Consistency, Reciprocation, Social Proof, Authority, Liking, and Scarcity.

As we go through these six principles, think about how you might use them in Infosec going forward.

(Commitment and) Consistency

Humans are amazingly consistent, even when it seems illogical. Once humans have made a commitment, regardless of how small, they tend to stick with it. Ever see someone who regularly does something that doesn't serve them well or someone in a horrible situation they won't remedy? That's because humans are consistent.

Once we have people doing the right thing, it is much easier to keep them doing the right thing, whether that is using good passwords, not letting people "tailgate" in the doors, doing source code reviews, or following change control procedures properly. Paying or somehow bribing them to do the right thing does not work; they know why they are doing it. They need to willingly do the right thing.

The more public a commitment, the stronger it is.

Accepting a job is a significant public commitment. Getting married is an even bigger one. That is why people may be in a horribly inappropriate job for themselves for years. That is why people have miserable marriages that last decades. Humans are absurdly consistent at times.

Also, small commitments can lead to bigger commitments (the "foot in the door" principle). Can you get someone to make a small commitment to security, and then leverage that?

Once we have small commitments to security it's easier to attain progressively larger commitments.

Reciprocation

If you do something nice for someone else, they are more likely to do something nice for you. Anthropologists claim this pervades all human societies, permeates exchanges of all kinds, and is actually the basis of human society.

This is why chimpanzees and other apes buy dinner, flowers, and open doors for other chimpanzees they are sexually interested in. Another example is how President Lyndon Johnson was incredibly effective. He got members of Congress, even those strongly opposed to various bills, to vote for and ratify them. How did he do this? He had done many favors for members of Congress during his many years in powerful positions in the house and senate.

Even something unwanted or uninvited can trigger the power of reciprocation. Those return address labels you don't order but come in the mail from people requesting donations definitely increases the number of donations; trust me, direct mail practitioners (i.e. junk mail pros) test these things extensively. They have metrics up the wazoo, i.e. extensive metrics.

Do you think there might be something we can learn from this that might help us be effective in our jobs? Are there ways you or your security program can add value to people and help them out? Maybe you can even experiment with giving them things they may or may not want, like mouse pads with security slogans or posters on security awareness.

Social Proof

When people are uncertain about what to do, they look to see what others are doing to guide their actions. This is called social proof.

We are herd animals to some extent, and social proof, essentially following the herd, is amazingly powerful. Most of us are not sheep, but we share some characteristics!

Ever notice that some people are popular just because they are popular (think back to high school if you have to), and some things are popular just because they are? If you have a beautiful boyfriend, girlfriend, etc. people are more likely to think you are attractive. If a place is popular, it must be good. And if McDonald's has sold 77 gadzillion hamburgers, they must be good. These are all examples of social proof.

If we can show that people are following our security policies and otherwise doing the right thing security wise, others will more easily follow. One way to help do this is to make positive examples of people, highlighting them doing the right things in your organization.

Authority

People follow authority, even those who claim they hate authority. There is both positional authority (e.g. the boss, the program manager) and personal authority (e.g. the person really in charge, the very likable and influential person in no official position of authority, the popular person everyone follows, etc.). People follow both types of authorities.

In ISO 27002 (formerly ISO17799 formerly BS 7799), The ISMS (Information Security Management System) statement is very effective. It is a statement by senior executives (the CEO works very well) saying security is important, or more formally, that security is important to business operations and senior management supports a culture of security. Why? An authority, hopefully the CEO (*the* authority) is suggesting you comply.

Can you get an endorsement or somehow align yourself with an authority? Can you get buy-in for your programs and initiatives from someone with authority? It can be very powerful if you can.

Liking

If people like you, they are more likely to do what you want them to. We prefer to say yes to people we like.

Research shows we tend to like people like us. Any similarity will do. It could be a common background, sport, hobby, favorite food, or where we originally came from. Sales people often look for similarities as part of the sales process to help influence you to buy, and so can you.

Research also shows attractive people are more likeable. While there is absolutely a genetic component to attractiveness as well as a "physical" component (for example, not being five hundred pounds overweight), much of how physical attractiveness is perceived is based on how we dress and groom ourselves. This is true for both men and women, although men consider raw physical attractiveness somewhat more.

We also like people we eat with. A lot of business discussions and negotiations are carried out over food, because it makes it easier to reach an agreement as we grow to like the people we are eating with.

Compliments (as long as they are not obviously shallow or vapid, in other words real compliments) increase liking.

We also like people connected with good news. Some cultures actually killed messengers who brought bad news and rewarded messengers who brought good news.

Be nice. Be likeable. Look for commonalities with others. Compliment where appropriate. Try to connect yourself with good.

Scarcity

The fear of loss, of missing out, is a powerful motivator. If something is scarce, it is perceived by the human mind as more valuable. Something could be scarce because there is a deadline after which it is unavailable, because only a limited number are available, or both.

Statements like "Order before midnight tonight," and "Supplies are limited," really do work. They help influence people to take action.

The restaurant that is difficult to get a reservation at must be better than the one you can easily get into. Really? No, but that's how the human mind works. If reservations are difficult to get, we tend to think they are more valuable.

When I was selling an educational program online, sometimes after a teleseminar or other presentation, I'd bundle an hour of "free" coaching/consulting for the first few people to buy my program. Obviously, my time is limited; it is reasonable I only offer a free hour to a limited number of people. It increased sales significantly. It influenced people to sign up.

The first time I ran my Infosec Rock Star online class it only had a few spots available, which helped make it seem more valuable. In fact, it *did* make it more valuable; several people expressed surprise that I responded to all personal emails in detail; obviously that kind of personal attention would be impossible if there were two hundred participants. When I run my class now, enrollment is only open for a few days, and guess what? Most people sign up on the absolute last day enrollment is open; yes, most people sign up when scarcity kicks in.

How do you use scarcity in Infosec? The answer as always is, "It depends," and it does depend on the organization. As an independent consultant, it is easy for me. I have limited time. For example, sometimes I can start a project for a client now or in a few weeks, but after that I may not be available for a while.

Leadership

Rock Stars are leaders. That doesn't necessarily mean you are a manager or want to be. A leader is simply anyone who has followers, and I often use the term *fans*, as you know. Leadership has not fundamentally changed; however, the Internet opens new leadership opportunities. Depending on your Future Orientation, your *Why*, or your personal mission statement, this may be significant. It is possible to reach more people easily than ever before, as well as geographically disparate groups of people that couldn't practically be reached previously.

Leaders have authority. There is both positional authority, which depends on position, power, or title, and personal authority. So what exactly is personal authority?

We all know that sometimes the real person (or people) in charge in any scenario is not the positional leader, but someone else without a title or the corner office or position on the organizational chart. This is someone who is well known and respected and who is really in charge. They have personal authority.

Ideally, a positional leader also has personal authority. You can have positional authority because you are "the boss," or "the CEO," or "a General," or maybe you have the guns and badges. Positional authority is most effective when combined with personal authority. Personal authority is earned. It is based on your standing with others. It is based on trust and respect.

Obviously *being an authority*, as in the "Survive->Stable->Expert->Authority->Rock Star" progression, and *having authority*, are not exactly the same but are very related. Experts will commonly have some authority, Authorities will certainly, and Rock Stars absolutely!

Action Step: Leadership for Everybody

Make sure you go to http://infosecrockstar.com/bonuses/ and get the extra training videos and resources that go along with this book.

In particular, watch the video on Leadership for Everyone.

Rock Stars Are Leaders

Leadership is a mindset, not a position. Rock Stars have a leadership mindset.

Maybe people change something they do or modify how they do it simply because you set a good example. Maybe they often order what you do at restaurants because you have great taste. Maybe they get you to order wine for the table because you can decipher a wine list well. Maybe they start shaving their heads because you did first, or maybe because you are "the boss" and they have to. It doesn't matter why people follow you; if they follow you, you are by definition a leader.

We will discuss both personal authority, and to a lesser degree positional authority. Rock Stars have personal authority, authority which is earned by providing value. They may or may not have positional authority.

Again, leaders have followers. If a leader has personal authority, their followers are fans. If a leader has merely positional authority, they merely have followers, not fans. A fan follows willingly; they do not follow just because they have to.

Characteristics of Leaders

Most organizations of any size describe leadership competencies they use to help identify and develop future leaders, and help improve current up and coming leaders. Some organizations may define dozens of leadership competencies, some ten or less; there is no agreed upon list of competencies but lots of similarities between different lists.

> *"Leadership competencies are leadership skills and behaviors that contribute to superior performance."*
> – Society for Human Resource Management.[14]

Common Leadership Competencies include Vision/Strategy, Ethics, Self-Direction, Project Management, Professionalism, Influence/Negotiating, Team Building, Managing Change, Political Skills, Decision Making, Stable Personal Life, and Inspirational.

Notice that we have discussed a great many of these leadership competencies. Although these are all valuable skills or qualities to possess, we have concentrated on the ones most valuable, in some

---

14 "Leadership Competencies." *Society for Human Resource Management.* March 01, 2008. Accessed December 20, 2016. https://www.shrm.org/resourcesandtools/hr-topics/behavioral-competencies/leadership-and-navigation/pages/leadershipcompetencies.aspx.

cases arguably essential, for personal authority, and all Rock Stars have personal authority.

Leading Without Knowing

You may have leadership experience and not even know it. It is possible to lead without knowing. I never thought of the following as an example of leadership, but it is (I honestly hadn't thought about it in decades.).

In 1986 at Apollo Computer, I was writing a system administration class for their Unix-like system (Domain/IX). I was to model it on the administration class for Domain/OS, their main operating system. A lot of the class was very similar. I decided that we simply needed to cover TCP/IP, which was not remotely widespread at the time, as well as system hardening issues, to add more value for the people who would be taking the class. As a recent college graduate who was very new to the full-time workforce, of course I discussed this with my boss. He had concerns, but I convinced him (think negotiation and influence) that it was not only the right thing to do, but that I could effectively do it, which meant staying on schedule and still covering everything else important.

Did anyone follow my initiative? Absolutely. Customers loved it. I did need to position the information in the course as useful and valuable, which was not immediately obvious to most, but which was to me.

Clearly this was an example of personal authority, which I was developing rapidly within this organization.

If you think back, I'll bet most, if not all, of you have led with knowing at some point in your past.

Leadership is About Taking Initiative

Leadership is about taking initiative. Taking initiative is relatively rare, but it doesn't need to be. You do not need to be "ordained" or somehow chosen. All you need is passion and ideas. There is no shortage of ideas. Even people who think themselves the most common and maybe even boring have great ideas. Ideas that spread, win. If you have an idea and do nothing with it or take no initiative, it doesn't matter much because it's not going to spread. Ideas involve change, and change scares many people.

I loves how Seth Godin says not to ask, "What is a risk-free way to insinuate myself into the system so I get approval to make the change?"[15] That simply is not possible.

You can simply start leading by setting a great example. When people follow your example, you *are* leading.

Conversely, you may choose not to lead, at least not now, at least not in some areas. It might not be the right time, or the right cause, or whatever. But there is rarely a "perfect" time for anything.

Leaders Versus Managers

A great leader does the right things.

Leaders take initiative. People follow great leaders; not because they have to, but because they want to. Of course, a leader can also be a manager because of where they are on the organizational chart.

A great manager does things right.

A manager may or may not take initiative (in other words, be a leader). They have subordinates and manage them to help insure they do their jobs properly. Management is the practice of compliance.

---

15   Godin, Seth. *Tribes: we need you to lead us.* London: Piatkus, 2008.

Great leaders inspire people to action. Managers tell people what to do.

Management is important. Without good management, planes do not fly on time, the supermarket shelves are not stocked, and your favorite bar may be out of beer.

Management and Leadership Are Different Things

Someone can be a great manager without being a leader, as well as a great leader without being a manager.

Think of the manager of an assembly line. Their job is one of compliance, of assuring those they manage, their subordinates, do their jobs and do them right. Their job is not to take initiative. They cannot change how the assembly line works, or what it produces, or make any other significant changes.

Often but not always, leaders are managers. It is very possible for someone to have both roles, yet only be good at one, as they are very different. For example, Steve Jobs was recognized by most as a great leader, yet many thought he was a horrific manager.

In the last few years I've led several projects; however, I was not a manager. I had no direct reports, I took initiative to do what was needed to make the projects successful. Of course others worked on the projects, and I hopefully inspired them to do their jobs well. I'm pretty sure I did most of the time. However, they didn't report to me; I didn't give them their periodic reviews, I had no official power over them, and I couldn't directly make them do anything.

Leadership – Studied Forever

Leadership is a subject that humans have studied for thousands of years, and "The study of leadership can be dated back to Plato, Sun Tzu and Machiavelli"[16] according to Wikipedia.

16   "Leadership studies." *Wikipedia.* Wikimedia Foundation, Accessed December 20, 2016. https://en.wikipedia.org/wiki/Leadership_studies.

Knowing how to lead and the art of leadership are two different things. You can learn a lot about leadership from the many great and valuable resources on leadership available, but you can't learn to lead without doing it.

You only learn to lead by taking initiative and leading. And the best leaders work hard at becoming better leaders. Leadership is something that can't be mastered in a lifetime.

I love to fly fish, a sport roughly as frustrating as golf, I'm told. I get to visit beautiful places I'd never see otherwise, like a full moon on Paris Flats on Christmas Island; The Marquesas twenty miles west of Key West; and sunrise on little unnamed and obscure creeks not far from home.

There are tons of instructional videos and more on learning how to fly fish and mastering fly fishing, probably something that can't be accomplished in a lifetime. And as good as many of those resources are, you really only learn to fly fish by doing it.

Similarly, you can study leadership forever, but unless you start leading you won't develop any leadership skills.

The Internet Changes (almost) Everything

Let me be clear about this: there are more opportunities for leadership than ever before in the history of the human race. *Everyone* can be a leader – no, not the Supreme Leader of Elbonia or North Korea or whatever, but everyone can lead where they have passion and ideas. And we *all* have ideas.

The Internet eliminates geography; it's easy and cheap to communicate with your fans and potential fans anywhere. There is a myriad of ways that didn't exist until recently to gather fans and to coordinate and communicate with people.

Let that sink in for a moment. The Internet eliminates geography, and it is now easy and cheap to communicate with your fans and potential fans anywhere. Leadership principles haven't changed but communications with fans, those who may willingly follow you, has.

I am not focusing only on social media here. For example, a good opt-in email list of fans is incredibly powerful for example (in fact, one email address is worth ten to twenty Facebook friends or more).

Of course you may want to lead locally; globally may not be your concern and that is fine as well.

Are Leaders . . .

There are many theories in the study of leadership. These theories apply to leaders with both positional and/or personal authority.

Some believe that great leaders are born. They are born to lead and are innately good leaders. Although debatable, I agree that some people are born with leadership skills, whether realized or not.

Some people choose to become leaders. Leadership can be learned. As we said before, leadership has been studied for a long time, for millennia, and we can learn from those studies. Can someone who is not a born leader learn to become as good a leader as someone born to lead? That is a great question with no agreed upon answer.

People also can be chosen to lead. They may be the logical and best choice, perhaps an awesome choice, even if they do not recognize this themselves. They may be chosen by others, or it may be circumstances that cause them to be chosen. They may be chosen by circumstances because there is a leadership void, and simply doing their job or doing what is right requires them to assume leadership.

Anyone can be a leader, and many of us are whether we realize it or not.

You *Can* Choose to Lead

Anyone can choose to lead. You do not need permission. You cannot assume positional authority, although you can build and earn personal authority through your actions.

One reason you may do this is there may be a lack of leadership. I love this quote by Kenneth G. Hartman below.

"A leadership vacuum is an indication that you need to step up and lead. Don't wait for permission!"
– Kenneth G. Hartman

Rock Stars Are Leaders

Rock Stars have earned Personal Authority by providing value to their fans. They may or may not have Positional Authority, and may not want it!

Sometimes as a Rock Star you may need to try to get your fans to take specific actions.

As a concrete example, I used all kinds of influence techniques to get people into my Rock Star class the first time. My goal was to get a very small group of people together who could add value to the material which has formed the basis of this book, and who could help me make the class better. I feel I succeeded quite well so far. Not perfectly – that doesn't exist! If I waited for perfect, the class would have never started and this book would never have been finished.

After the first running of the class, I still used all kinds of influence techniques, both positive and negative. For example, I stated quite strongly and multiple times exactly who the class was designed for and who it was not. I stated, "Infosec Rock Star is firmly targeted for those from mid-level Stable, where you already have some expert Geek skills but may not have expert positioning, on up to Expert and Authority, and concentrates on understanding and learning the skills necessary to be a Rock Star." I didn't tell anyone they couldn't take the course, but I did use positive and negative influence techniques.

Most importantly, I took initiative. Many well-meaning friends told me, sometimes quite literally, that I was crazy; I'll admit I hear that somewhat often because of my somewhat wild and creative persona.

Most creative thoughts and ideas initially seem crazy to most, including the most successful ones. Ideas such as, "An online book store; that will never work, people want to pick up and see the books," and "Index the Internet for free? How will you possibly make money doing that?" are ideas that seemed crazy at the time to most. The founders no doubt had to convince people, including their fans, to help. Amazon and Google are obviously wildly successful today.

Your fans will love your ideas. Not necessarily all of them, not necessarily immediately, but in general they will love them.

5
INFOSEC, SALARY, AND MONEY

●　●　●　●　●　●　●

Money matters.

It would be nice if it didn't. Once upon time, it didn't for me. I was a hardworking geek getting paid well for doing what I loved. I took a trip of a lifetime at least once a year, I ate and drank extremely well, saw lots of live music, but generally lived a fairly simple life. Money was numbers in accounts. The numbers were always good. Then I had kids. The amount of money I needed increased dramatically.

Money means different things to different people. Some people don't even care about money. For others, money seems to be their main driver in life. To me, money represents freedom. Freedom is one of the biggest driving forces in my life.

Making money for working, also known as trading time for money, is but one model. It's not a bad one for most people.

One can also start a company. Or develop and sell valuable intellectual property. And there are plenty of opportunities for overlap. You might be an employee with a great salary, maybe including equity, at a startup. And startups often have or develop intellectual property. Or you may be recognized as a Rock Star at your company because you have developed some critical intellectual property for them. And there are plenty of other possible permutations as well.

Salary/Pay

Most people are employees, and the first thing they think of is salary or pay. We'll discuss this first, but make sure you keep an open mind as we go forward.

The concepts here apply to employees as well as contractors. They also apply to consultants, although consultants often have more flexibility.

More at

http://infosecrockstar.com/bonuses/ on the differences and benefits of the employee, consultant, and contractor models.

It *is* possible to have an enormous salary or be paid phenomenally well as a contractor or consultant if you are a Rock Star. This is relatively rare for technical people, although possible. Let's look at people that often make enormous salaries.

Why do CEOs and Other Executives Often Have Enormous Salaries?

Some people, such as CEOs, have enormous salaries. At the risk of starting a quasi-political fight, let's discuss this.

Why are their salaries so high? Reasons certainly include that skilled CEOs and other executives are in demand; it's very possible they bring that much value to the organization and are worth it, and they may also negotiate salary well.

Many people believe some salaries are obscene. Perhaps some are. No doubt some CEOs and other executives are overpaid. So are some bus drivers, mechanics, fortune tellers, system administrators, MacOS forensic examiners, and CPAs. I define *overpaid* as paid more than the value they create, which is no doubt difficult to determine and subject to debate.

Steve Jobs, in his return to Apple, brought Apple back from almost ten years of plummeting sales. In March 1997, Apple had a quarterly loss of $708 million. Then Jobs returned and brought Apple back. What is that worth? Obviously a lot.

If a CEO adds $10 billion in value to a company, or positions them for enormous growth in the future through strategic investments in perhaps R&D and personnel, or prevents a bad situation from being much worse, what is that worth? Again, obviously a lot.

Average Infosec Salaries

By definition, most people make an average salary, not a Rock Star salary, and average salaries in our field can be awesome. It is easy to find average salary information online. For example, the following below are from the Infosec Institute[17] and from the SANS Salary Survey,[18] and there are several other sources like the Robert Half® Salary Guides.[19]

17 *Information Technology Training and Bootcamps*. Infosec Institute. Retrieved December 20, 2016, from https://www.infosecinstitute.com/

18 *Cybersecurity Professional Trends: A SANS Survey*. SANS Information Security Training | Cyber Certifications | Research. Arbor Networks, May 2014. Web. 20 Dec. 2016. <https://www.sans.org/reading-room/whitepapers/analyst/cybersecurity-professional-trends-survey-34615>.

19 *Robert Half Salary Guides*. Robert Half. Robert Half, 2016. Web. 20 Dec. 2016. <https://www.roberthalf.com/workplace-research/salary-guides>.

- [ ] Median CISSP Salary, Boston: US$103,520
- [ ] CISO/CSO, 0-3 years' experience, US$89,500
- [ ] CISO/CSO, 20+years' experience, US$150,000
- [ ] Security Analyst, 4-6 years' experience, US$79,034

Of course none of these are perfect but they give us a reference point, and certainly certifications, education, experience, location, management, and leadership roles all affect salary.

Who Wants to be Average?

Hopefully no one reading this book wants to be average. The opposite of being average or generic is being a Rock Star and making a difference.

There *is* more to a job than just money. For example, I have done pro bono work. I also undertook one major project for a non-profit that I believed in for about 10 percent of what I'd charge others. I would have done it for free. And I have certainly left phenomenally great paying gigs because they were boring and not using my talents well.

> *"Being generic is a choice. If you are generic, a cog in the machine, you will always be struggling."*
> – Seth Godin

Being average or generic used to pay off, at least a generation back. You would get a job, work for a few decades fitting in as best you could, and then retire. There are not many places where this "job for life" is still true and even if it appears to be, beware. However, if you have a job at an organization you love and want to spend your career there, I envy you. I'm seriously jealous and hope it works out.

I don't want to have or do an average job or get average pay either. Do you?

Average, or even below average pay for an amazing job might be fine, but all other things being equal, higher pay is better than lower pay.

Two Pricing Models

We are going to look at two pricing models, Market Based Pricing and Value Based Pricing.

Market Based Pricing

We are all familiar with "Market Based Pricing." What does a cup of coffee cost? I paid $2.40 today for a great cup. What does a <Insert Job Role Here> cost? That is market based pricing.

For example, what is the market price of a CTO? According to *salary.com*, a CTO earns between $167K to $253K with a median salary of $206K. We should be able to get a very competent CTO in that price range.

Value Based Pricing

Let's say you are with a new security-based company and you have plenty of venture capital. Maybe you are going to try to hire Dr. Eric Cole or Bruce Schneier or Brian Krebs or another high visibility Rock Star, perhaps as the CTO. The market price of CTOs doesn't matter much here. What matters is how much value they will add to the company. Even just having their name associated with your company will potentially add massive value, not to mention having their smarts and skills. The potential salary and perks will depend on the value they add to your company.

I first heard of the concept of Value-Based Fees and Value-Based Pricing from Consulting Rock Star Alan Weiss in his book *Value-Based Fees: How to Charge - and Get - What You're Worth*. Although his book is aimed at consultants the concepts apply to all.

In order to get off the (market based) chart pricing, you need to be a Rock Star. With value based pricing, the focus is on output or outcomes, not inputs. If you can spend a day and add massive value, are you paid for a day's time or for the value you create? With value based pricing you are paid for the value. If many people could add that value in a day, then we are back to market pricing and getting paid for that day's work. You are not unique in this case, you are a commodity, although perhaps a valuable one, and not a Rock Star. Good news, however. Even approaching Rock Star, you can get well above-average money. How much depends on many factors.

Moving Toward Rock Star

Moving Toward Rock Star

Moving Toward Rock Star

Market Based Salary Range

Ultimate Rock Star Off The Chart Pay

You may never be the ultimate absolute Rock Star in your field, and that's ok. You may never achieve totally seemingly absurd, way off the chart, pay. Your salary may never be seven or eight figures, or you may never bill $1,000 an hour or more; that's fine.

However, as you move toward Rock Star, your salary will move to the edge of the market based salary range and beyond, if you provide enough unique value. It needs to be unique so that you are not a commodity. It needs to be massive value, so you are worth it.

The Startup Company

The standard employee or contractor or consultant model is not the only way to go.

The classic way to make lots of money in high tech is via a startup. I've been with several startups and love the excitement and chaos, but honestly it is not for everyone. Actually it is not for most people, which is not to dissuade anyone. Even as a non-founder, at the early stages, a great many people get stock options, which may be worth a small fortune. I've done well but never had any of my options amount to much.

My friend Big Company Barbara always worked for very large organizations. She thrived in those environments. At least one of those big companies was a very dynamic company with an entrepreneurial outlook. One day she asked me about a startup she was thinking of joining. After much discussion, I gave her my opinion: "Go for it, but I don't think you'll like it." She did, and found the experience valuable, but the chaos and disorganization drove her nuts. Startups are not for her.

What's a Startup?

We all have a basic idea of what a startup is, although we could debate the exact definition.

A startup could be in any business area and not high-technology focused, but for our purposes we will stick to technology oriented startups that have high growth potential. In addition, our working definition of startups includes "potentially innovative/disruptive."

So, we wouldn't consider a chain of new restaurants to be a startup; however, a chain of new restaurants that allowed you to order from your phone and delivered your food via a drone within ten minutes would qualify. A chain of bookstores wouldn't qualify, but *Amazon.com* did.

According to *Forbes.com* and others, 90 percent of startups fail; that's nine out of ten. I've been in failed startups before and I know a few others of us have as well. That doesn't mean the experience wasn't valuable. That doesn't mean you didn't learn and have fun and get paid. It just means the startup failed to reach its goals.

Different Startup Involvement Models

So, do you have a great idea for a startup? You may be one of the founders or perhaps one of the first onboard. In one startup, I wasn't a founder, but I was the fifth on board and helped refine and execute the idea. In another ongoing concern, I was a very early stage investor. I invested very low five figures to help them start and own some equity. In another startup I merely had an unpaid position on the board of advisors. If they had skyrocketed, there was certainly value in being on the board.

You can also be a rank-and-file employee in a startup. It is common to receive equity, perhaps stock options, and many fortunes have been made this way. There are plenty of secretaries and other relatively low-level employees who made millions. Look at Microsoft, for example. You may or may not receive lower pay in exchange for some equity. As a consultant, I've been offered equity several times in lieu of or as partial payment (side note: as a consultant this rarely works out in your favor in my experience).

You can learn an incredible amount very quickly as an employee in a startup, and that may be very cool. You may also find you are doing things you never imagined like buying office furniture, running the online marketing, hiring and firing, and much more you never signed on to do. This isn't necessarily bad; anything you learn is positive.

The Startup Life

Roles are definitely not well established at startups; they simply can't be. You do what needs to be done. The CEO may empty trash cans. Even lower-level employees may have strategic input.

If you enjoy doing what needs to be done and are focused on outcomes instead of inputs, this can be absolutely fantastic. If you only want to do what you specialize in, this may or may not work out. I happen to like business, I like startups, so although fundamentally a geek, I'm happy to figure out and execute business stuff, such as hacking procedures and whatever it takes to make things work well. My hacking is not confined to technology.

Things change quickly in startups. You had better love a dynamic and energetic environment. You might put in potentially crazy hours at times, although this is far less widespread than during the dot com boom. We do not see a lot of sleeping on and under desks as we did in the late '90s. However, do not expect a forty-hour workweek.

You are more important in a startup. Everyone's opinion is more valuable. The one startup I should have abandoned early had a CEO who refused to take input from anyone. I explained to the fool several times that he was not the real CEO and it was nearly certain he would be replaced by our venture capitalists by someone with a track record as a condition of our next round of financing, but that, like most other things, fell on deaf ears.

Funding

Businesses require resources, especially time and money. Most startups will need several rounds of funding. Rapid growth generally requires this. If a startup is doing well, that is growing extremely quickly, additional funding allows them (ideally) to invest so that rapid growth can be sustained or accelerated.

Bootstrapping means using existing resources; starting a business without external help or capital. Many people have bootstrapped companies using savings, with early employees working for little or no cash pay (although perhaps equity or similar), and reinvesting the (hopefully) quickly generated profits back into the business. Although I love bootstrapping, most businesses will grow faster with external funding.

Angel investors may be an option. Wikipedia describes an angel investor as "an affluent individual who provides capital for a business startup, usually in exchange for convertible debt or ownership equity."[20] Angel investors can include your parents, your neighbor, your Uncle Throckmorton, as well as someone who invests in many startups and has for a while as an angel investor. Make sure angel investors understand what is going on. You don't want your uncle wondering when he is getting interest because he isn't!

The venture capital route is common. Venture capitalists are companies or individuals that invest in startups, generally assuming an active role that can include providing managerial and technical expertise. Venture capitalists vary widely; some may invest in only a certain industry, new startups, or existing startups that need cash to continue rapid growth. Be careful; many, including myself, have had severe ethical issues with venture capitalists, hence the term "vulture capitalists." There are certainly plenty of great Venture Capitalists as well. Be selective with your venture capitalists.

Crowd sourcing is a newer funding technique. It is getting small monetary contributions from lots of people, often using the Internet.

---

20   "Angel investor." *Wikipedia*. Wikimedia Foundation, Web. 20 Dec. 2016.

The Business Plan

When looking for funding, you need a business plan. Please realize the business plan is primarily a marketing document. That does not mean it is fiction, but it portrays the best scenario possible, if things go perfectly. Commonly, people take reasonable financial projections and multiply them by ten, going from a great case scenario to an absurdly best case scenario. Who knows, they might make it. There is nothing unethical with portraying the best case possibly, but obvious lies and fabrications are clearly wrong. Know the difference.

Plans and planning are great, with the understanding that "No plan survives contact with reality." Even if bootstrapping, you should have a (written down) plan, not just ideas in your head.

Exit Strategies

How do the investors get their money out? Whether there are investors or not, how do you get yourself out? This is called the Exit Strategy.

Your investors will want their money back, hopefully with massive profits, at some point. That certainly includes venture capitalists as well as angel investors and others. Even if you bootstrap a company, you may have enormous wealth yet very little cash. An exit strategy is how to change illiquid assets like company ownership and stock into liquid assets like cash. Even if you do not plan on exiting the company, you may want to convert some assets to cash.

There are lots of possibilities, including selling the company, a management buyout, going public (an Initial Public Offering), and simply walking away when you are done or have had enough.

The most important thing about an exit strategy is having thought and planned before it's time.

The Sidepreneur Model

I'm not sure I like the term *sidepreneur*, but it's becoming more common, so let's use it.

Quite simply, this is doing your main gig with a side gig. Your main gig is commonly a fulltime job or contract or consulting in your field of expertise.

More than one company has been started on the side by an employee and gone on to compete directly. There is nothing wrong with getting your feet wet and then diving in if the water is nice, such as leaving your job to devote your time to your startup if it works out, but there can be ethical issues, including division of time and energy and conflict of interest. You may be violating noncompete agreements, employment agreements, or other agreements, written or implied.

In some cases there clearly are no issues. As examples, I have 2 Infosec friends heavily into real estate investing, another actively trading in the stock market, and yet another developing and selling software for a large hobby of his.

Summary: Money Matters

Money rocks. While there are plenty of things more important than money, such as love and health, it is fair to say most of us consider money to be a significant part of success. Many people have a love-hate relationship with money. Do you think money is evil? Do you hate rich people? Does seeing a Rolls-Royce or Ferrari make you angry?

Well then, you have negative thoughts and connotations about money. Chances are extremely high that you will never have much. This is exactly the same as (written from a guy's perspective) if you think that all beautiful women are stuck up and abuse men, then chances are you will never have a girlfriend or wife you consider beautiful.

Money is inanimate; it cannot be evil or good. No more than a pair of pliers, or a fence, or a rock can be evil or good. Money can be acquired in an evil way or used for evil purposes, otherwise it's great. Money can be used for wonderful purposes. It gives you the ability to do plenty of good.

Being able to write a check or pull out a credit card and make some problems go away is great. Of course you can't make all problems go away, but enough so that it makes having money great!

Warren Buffett, Bill Gates, and Mark Zuckerberg are giving billions to charity. Isn't it cool that they are doing that? Wouldn't it be cool if you could too?

Money itself can be a problem for some people, but ANYTHING can be a problem, including money.

To me, money represents freedom, and freedom is an enormous driver in my life. And the more you move toward Rock Star status, the more opportunities you have, including opportunities to make money.

6
OWN YOUR FUTURE: LIVING THE DREAM

· · · · · · ·

Longevity and Lifestyle

'm in this for the long run; how about you? I plan to keep improving, adding value to my communities, and living a fantastic and relatively healthy lifestyle. I plan to keep moving toward Rock Star.

We can all add value to our organization, our colleagues, our friends, and ourselves. We all have talents, developed and undeveloped. Unfortunately, a lot of incredibly talented people do not reach their potential. They may do great things for a while and then stop. In the field of Rock and Roll, they often die young. Is there much of a difference with a brilliant entrepreneur who does something amazing and then fades away, maybe retiring with a few million dollars and never doing much of consequence afterward, and a gifted musician who dies unnecessarily in his '20s?

Keith Richards is one of the greatest guitar players ever. He is certainly not a model to follow closely, but he has survived a long time, has always given back, has always created value, and is simply unpretentious and always himself. He's also been expelled for truancy, has several drugs arrests, and has had a life full of controversy. Musical journalists have described him as "mad, bad, and dangerous to know"[21] (Nick Kent) and "a capering streak of living gristle who ought to be exhibited as a warning to the young of what drugs can do to you even if you're lucky enough not to choke on your own vomit"[22] (Peter Hitchens).

Yet Richards has been described as "direct, incisive, and unpretentious."[23] He has always credited artists who influenced him. He has always been willing to play with musicians who are his friends, who have inspired him, who have encouraged him. He's even friends with Justin Bieber, a young and popular musician who seems about as opposite to Keith Richards musically and otherwise as possible. He has been making great music for over fifty years both with the Rolling Stones and others.

He has always created value. He has always given back. That is worth celebrating about him.

Continually Moving Toward Rock Star

You are going to see a lot of change as our field, society, and the world rapidly changes; much of this change is driven by technology. Even if this were not true, change is constantly occurring; it is inevitable.

You want to be continually moving toward Rock Star, even if you are already considered a Rock Star by others. We want changes

21   Bockris, Victor. *Keith Richards: the biography*. New York: Poseidon Press, 1992. Print. Page 213.
22   Goldstein, Jack, and Frankie Taylor. *101 Amazing Rolling Stones Facts*. Luton: Andrews UK Limited, 2012. Print.
23   "Keith Richards." *Wikipedia*. Wikimedia Foundation. Web. 25 Dec. 2016.

to be in this direction, guided by our Future Orientation as discussed in chapter one.

Change, if left to chance tends to be random. You are not going to suddenly wake up a Rock Star if you do the bare minimum at work, and then watch TV and drink Bud Lite every night and every weekend too. There is nothing wrong with TV (I watch it occasionally) or Bud Lite (although in my opinion it is tasteless industrial swill). If you are all about doing the minimum at work, TV, and Bud Lite, change will mainly be slow and random. If you are happy, more power to you, but you are probably not reading this if that is all you aspire to.

Now don't get me wrong: we all "coast" at periods in our lives. I certainly have and suspect at times I may have coasted too long and at times coasted too short!

The entire point of this book is positive evolution and transformation. Moving toward Rock Star! Becoming a better Rock Star! One enormous factor here is whether you are proactive or not; proactivity lends itself towards positive change.

"You is a very fluid concept."[24]
– *Hitch,* the movie

You absolutely *is* a very fluid concept. We are all capable of and probably doing things we couldn't imagine just a few years ago, although we probably don't think of them or maybe even realize them. I never imagined I'd ever be writing a book and teaching classes on anything with "Rock Star" in the title, entering physical endurance events, or traveling the world and getting paid for it.

---

24   *Hitch.* Dir. Andy Tennant. By Kevin Bisch. Perf. Will Smith. Columbia, 2005.

Change/Evolution

I'm not the person I was six months or two years ago, and neither should you be. Change is inevitable, so embrace it, direct it, channel it.

Although my friends from college and before often say, "You haven't changed at all," and my essential core (however one may define that) is the same, I *am* a very different person. I've learned a lot since college and it has positively changed me. Change isn't always positive, and one can be worse off and grow extremely bitter and negative with age as well, even when things are going superbly.

One of the reasons for Future Orientation is to try, to some extent, to channel change in positive directions you choose. Of course you do not have total control, but you do have significant influence.

There is a common yet sad story of someone who leaves, perhaps a job or a home and stops regularly hanging out with a group of friends. They return a few years later, and nothing has changed. Everyone is the same; they do the same things, and as far as you can tell they are even wearing the same clothes.

Change for the sake of change is not necessarily good (although companies sometimes do it to shake things up and avoid complacency). If you love fishing or watching football or eating chicken wings, there is no reason to change that. However, if in ten or twenty years your life hasn't changed at all, it is worth examining your life in some detail.

I have friends who are mentally still in high school or college. Not much has changed. If they're happy, I'm happy for them, but this doesn't describe me and it probably doesn't describe you.

Action Step: Review your Personal Mission Statement or *Why*.

Remember in chapter one we wrote a preliminary Personal Mission Statement or *Why* to use to guide our high-level decision making and used the term *Future Orientation*. *Future Orientation* helps guide our change.

Review, and if appropriate (and you're ready) make some changes. This may require thinking about it for a while; at least review it for now.

Rapid Change: Punctuated Equilibrium and Quantum Change

Change can be very rapid. A hit record, a new relationship, a new job, a meteorite killing dinosaurs. So let's say your wife throws you out of the house (permanently), you take up heavy drinking (temporarily), start dating the babysitter (probably temporarily), and get a new job or contract; that's four very positive things (potentially). That, my friend, is rapid change.

Punctuated Equilibrium and Quantum Change

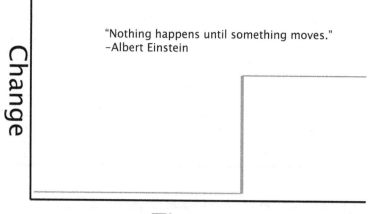

Punctuated Equilibrium and Quantum Change…Google them if you'd like. Punctuated Equilibrium is a theory from evolution that states change is usually is slow to non-existent, a state called stasis. When significant change (rarely) occurs, it tends to be rapid.

Rapid change might occur because you learn or master a new skill. As a simple example, my daughter at six years of age went from two years of skiing as a timid beginner to being able to ski the entire mountain with ease in about two weeks. It was a combination of confidence and skills development. It was definitely rapid change. Her mother was shocked. I was not; I taught her!

If you are Joe or Josephine Minimum Work/TV/Bud Lite, change will usually be slow to nonexistent, but will occasionally be significant and possibly disastrous.

Quantum Change is Punctuated Equilibrium on steroids. Massive changes quickly. Often adapt or die. Rock Stars thrive during Quantum Change. Others may or may not.

Think of a salt water clam living in an estuary that suddenly gets cut off from the sea and must live in fresh water or die.

Our Field is Changing Rapidly

If you want a job where things stay the same and your daily routine never changes, you are in the wrong field.

Just keeping up is challenging. What has been true for a long time suddenly becomes no longer true. That older knowledge or experience is still quite valuable, even though the facts may have changed, and learning the new is critical. The mindset useful when I was hacking PDP-11s and other ancient computers hasn't changed; the techniques have.

Lifelong learning is important. No, that's not quite right. In our field, lifelong learning is essential.

Lifelong Learning

Staying current is important, although we cannot stay current in the traditional sense. The body of human knowledge is simply growing too quickly. You can't stay current on *all* of Infosec or even *all* of Pen testing or *all* of Forensics.

Specialization is becoming more and more important, yet it is also very important to have a broad knowledge base. We very often end up doing things we never would have expected. I do a lot of high level Cyber Defense work, yet I never would have imagined I would have clients at which I didn't spend most of my time at the keyboard. The last eighteen months I've spent an incredible amount of time teaching and loving it, and I did not even know this was possible when I started in computers. Sometimes you find a specialization, sometimes it finds you.

There are Many Learning Options

The number of learning options, including one hundred percent free ones, has absolutely exploded. There are lots of paid options, including very expensive ones, which are also very worthwhile and provide extreme value.

Many organizations reward those who invest in themselves through learning, whether it's formally or informally. Even if you are a contractor or consultant, your clients may reward or look favorably on you.

We are going to look at some of the most popular options available.

Podcasts, Blogs, Newsletters

There are many fantastic free podcasts, blogs, and newsletters. I suggest you find ones you enjoy. I jump around and like to get info from different sources periodically. Here are some I always seem to come back to.

"*SANS NewsBites* is a semiweekly, high-level executive summary of the most important news articles that have been published on computer security during the last week. Each news item is very briefly summarized and includes a reference on the web for detailed information, if possible."[25] – from *sans.org*. In five to ten minutes, I'm able to keep up with all the Infosec news. I read *SANS NewsBites* regularly. https://www.sans.org/newsletters/newsbites

Paul's Security Weekly is always informative and amusing, and sometimes off the wall. Formerly known as *Paul Dot Com*. I've known Paul and his crew forever. http://securityweekly.com

Risky Business. "Lighthearted look at information security news and features" from Patrick Gray in Australia. http://risky.biz

---

25   "Newsletters: Newsbites." *SANS Institute | Newsletters - Newsbites*. The SANS Institute, Web. 20 Dec. 2016.

Schneier on Security, with Bruce Schneier really needs no introduction. I interviewed him once for a book on his strange habit of blogging about squid, the creature, every Friday. Hey, we are all a little strange, definitely including Bruce. https://www.schneier.com

Coursera

"Coursera provides universal access to the world's best education, partnering with top universities and organizations to offer courses for anyone to take, for free."[26]

Simply put, Coursera rocks. I've just finished a Crypto course from Stanford and am planning on part II soon, hopefully a music course from the Berklee College of Music, and an *Introduction to Public Speaking* course from the University of Washington. Yes, I do lots of public speaking but am always looking to improve, and yes, I know crypto pretty well but can certainly learn much more. They have classes available in many languages.

Cybrary

Cybrary launched in January of 2015 and they say, "Our goal is to provide the opportunity to learn Cyber Security, to anyone, anywhere, who wants that opportunity."[27] They have free online courses, forums, and a job board, among other things. Some of the classes look absolutely great, although I haven't taken any myself yet.

MIT OpenCourseWare

MIT OpenCourseWare is phenomenal and includes courses from the MIT Sloan School of Management. Besides technical courses,

---

26 "Online Courses From Top Universities. Join for Free." *Coursera*. Web. 20 Dec. 2016.
27 "Online Cyber Security Training, Free, Forever." *Cybrary*. Web. 20 Dec. 2016.

some interesting ones include Power and Negotiations and several courses on leadership. There is even a curious experimental course called Increasing Your Physical Intelligence, Enhancing Your Social Smarts.

Udemy

Udemy has all kinds of classes, most of which are quite inexpensive. They include classes by some Rock Stars like Guy Kawasaki and Seth Godin. I have taken some great ones from Udemy. A hint with Udemy is to Google for Udemy coupons and you can often take any course at a significant discount.

More Options

Of course there are lots of commercial offerings. I'm partial to SANS classes since, among other things, they help pay my bills and I teach several of their classes. There are plenty of other great offerings out there, depending on what you are looking for.

Blackhat and other 'cons are other great sources of information, sometimes including formal classes as well as great information in more common short conference type presentations.

Many organizations sponsor onsite classes and yours may.

Blue Jean Friday Afternoons

Often we lose our technical edge as our career progresses. For example, I rarely write code anymore. I have clients whose computers I have never touched (inconceivable to me a mere few years ago). I got the concept of "Blue Jean Friday Afternoons" from Stephen Northcutt who in turn got it from one of his mentors. Take the occasional Friday afternoon (when often not much happens), and dig into something technical you either haven't done before or haven't in a while. Get your hands dirty again.

For example, late last night I scanned my home network with Nmap and found some strange things. Turns out they were my children's devices, many of which were archaic, and I had no idea they were IP enabled. Last week I actually used my soldering iron for the first time in a while to repair an electronic device (just the cord; it was simple). I may be taking a Python programming course with my thirteen-year-old daughter if she can free up some busy time in her schedule. I also hacked an Internet connected treadmill and apparently I ran five hundred miles in ten minutes.

To Rock Long Term You Need ...

. . . to take care of yourself!

The Million Dollar Racehorse Analogy

If you had a million-dollar racehorse, you would make sure it ate healthily, exercised, and got adequate rest.

Do the same for yourself. You are more important than a horse. Try to eat healthily, exercise, and get enough sleep. Peak performance, certainly long term, depends on it.

I try, which is much better than not trying at all. I exercise, usually eat healthily, and am pretty fit and healthy. I couldn't go climb a major mountain or run a marathon without some preparation, but I can outdo many people half my age, and I'm no natural athlete.

Society has advanced to where we can be unhealthy and still survive. Medicine and social services, among other things, keep people alive that would have certainly perished in the wild, and mostly perished in earlier societies. There was no blood pressure medicine, high cholesterol medicine, heart bypasses, and social services depended on friends and family; you pretty much had to take care of yourself. Not that long ago, when my father was in medical school, we didn't even have antibiotics. My father remembered that well.

I propose that people who are relatively healthy and productive are happier people. I know I certainly am. And long term Rock Stars absolutely tend to be relatively healthy (see my upcoming lists of dead and alive) and productive.

To Rock Long Term You Also Need ...

. . . to be happy! Although I have zero medical or psychological expertise ... let's go:

What things in life make you happy? This is fairly personal and individual. You might not like visiting foreign lands, learning new languages, lifting weights, fly fishing, fine wines, public speaking, cooking, noisy children, cycling, or the beach like I do. These make me happy.

Certainly a positive attitude can help. Life always has its ups and downs; it's supposed to. There is always a reason to be happy. There is always a reason to be unhappy. Attitude matters.

Sex and Drugs

The most common questions I get in my live events are always on sex and drugs; maybe that shouldn't be a surprise but it has been to me. Certainly sex and drugs are mentally associated with rock and roll, and can also make people very happy or very unhappy, so here we go . . .

Sex (and Relationships)

If you are with someone who drags you constantly down, that is a total mismatch, or even worse, it will be next to impossible to do great things in your life.

Most humans are monogamous, or at least mostly monogamous, and most of us end up with a long term mate, whether we use the term partner, significant other, spouse, husband, or wife. (Note: The following is from a Western viewpoint. There are of course many different cultures in the world.)

This is possibly the most important choice you will make in your life. Yet most of us do not choose. We might think we do, but at some point in our lives our brains decide we should settle down, and we end up stuck with whomever we happened to be with at the time. And they end up stuck with us. That's what seems to happen most commonly.

This isn't necessarily bad, but it isn't necessarily great.

Most of us need to sort through a lot of people to find someone suitable. Not everyone is as lucky as a couple of my friends who are still happily married to their first ever boyfriend or girlfriend.

Dating skills are important. No one probably ever taught you how. It is not hard to learn. And similarly, being in a relationship, even the best possible, requires work. It's amazing how humans will put lots of time into hobbies and interests but close to zero into their relationships after the beginning . . . Whenever in doubt, take Bill and Ted's advice from *Bill & Ted's Excellent Adventure*: "Be excellent to each other."[28]

May I suggest simply living a fantastic life, and when you meet potentially the right person, inviting them in? Of course I also suggest being proactive, like with everything else.

Drugs, Legal and Beyond

To rock long term, to use the vernacular, you need to have your shit together. You need to take care of yourself. And I mean that on all fronts, including consumption.

28   *Ted and Bill's Excellent Adventure*. Dir. Stephen Herek. Perf. Keanu Reeves, Alex Winter, George Carlin . Orion Pictures, 1989. Film.

Here are three lists of musical Rock Stars:

Alive and Clean: Elton John, Eric Clapton, Ringo Starr, Tom Waits, Alice Cooper, Ted Nugent, James Hetfield, Eminem, Shania Twain, Mike Ness, 50 Cent, Fatboy Slim, Steven Tyler (maybe)

Dead, Permanently, Part I: Jimi Hendrix, Amy Winehouse, John Bonham, Ron "Pigpen" McKernan, Jim Morrison, Bon Scott

Dead, Permanently, Part II: Elvis Presley, Keith Moon, Sid Vicious, Janis Joplin, Brian Jones, Hank Williams, Sr., Tommy Dorsey, John Entwhistle, Kurt Cobain, Michael Jackson, Billie Holiday, John Kahn, Dee Dee Ramone, Prince

The *Alive and Clean* list are people who are taking care of themselves and not doing any illegal drugs. The *Dead* lists are obviously people who didn't take care of themselves.

By the way, the first *Dead* list, from Jimi Hendrix to Bon Scott, is from alcohol. Yes, my second favorite drug can kill if not handled with care and respect.

Παν μέτρον άριστον is an ancient Greek saying meaning, "Everything in moderation." For many substances, moderation means "avoid." Even ignoring illegalities, there are some substances few humans can handle. Did you know, for example, that humans can increase their tolerance to heroin by one hundred times in twenty-four hours? One hundred times, not one hundred percent, and of course it can and does kill, as well as being highly addictive.

I do not use illegal drugs. I don't use many legal drugs either. I'm not telling anyone else what to do, however, and I'm certainly not judging anyone.

Sex and Drugs, Part II

Can I simply say "Yes: Women, Alcohol, Caffeine"?

Remember, Παν μέτρον άριστον – everything in moderation.

I drink. Not daily, sometimes not even weekly, but I like alcohol, especially Grower Champagnes and other wines. And when I drink, I want something awesome. I am more likely to take fifteen minutes or more to make an artisanal cocktail or open a Champagne I've researched, tracked down, bought, and I am fascinated to try, than to open a cheap beer in a can. Nothing against beer in cans.

I do drink coffee nearly daily: freshly roasted beans, ground immediately before brewing, usually in a French Press. I have coffee geek friends who think a $165 grinder is an entry level grinder; clearly I am not a coffee geek. Show me I can taste the difference and maybe I can be converted.

In terms of women, I do find intelligence very attractive. I don't necessarily find heavy drinking attractive, but apparently women who drink heavily like me. Hmmmm . . . maybe that says something about me?

Also, perhaps unlike the "Rock Star" stereotype, I'm simply not remotely promiscuous. Maybe if thousands of groupies were throwing themselves at me things would be different, but I doubt it. I meet lots of fun, attractive, intelligent women. Occasionally I'm impressed, and I'm not shy about letting them know when that happens. Eventually I'll settle down, but I'm no longer interested in hot fun girlfriends who aren't the right person, although that was fine when I suddenly and gracefully became single a few years back.

And I will add that I do wish we had more women in this currently male-dominated field. Men and women are quite different, and we both bring something different to this field. Fortunately, things are changing.

This may or may not be considered sexist or improper, but if I have a team of ten male geeks, I value the input of a woman more than another male regardless of how intelligent and talented they might be.

I find extreme value in diversity. For those of you that know me well, you'll recognize that in my extreme diversity of personal friends.

No "Dating for Geeks" but …

I didn't want to write this, but …. I've been asked by many dozens, if not hundreds, to do a dating for geeks thing. First of all, although many of us are geeks (I sure am), we are not merely geeks. Secondly, I do not consider myself remotely qualified for a multitude of reasons, including that what works for me probably won't work for you. However, becoming gracefully single in my forties and having lots of single female friends who confide in me and ask my opinion does give me an interesting and hopefully valuable viewpoint.

The most attractive quality to most humans is confidence. Men, stick with me; you probably disagree at this point but trust me. My (medically) morbidly obese and in my opinion horror show "friend" Harriet regularly has a hot young boyfriend who usually supports her. She has severe issues, so she can't keep a boyfriend or job or much of anything else long, but she has self-confidence, so apparently many men find her stunningly attractive. Personally, I think she's atrocious, but my opinion is only one of many, and as I'm perhaps unusually honest, she knows exactly what I think.

Also, no one is "out of your league." There are no leagues. This is a stupid concept brought on by a lack of confidence. You can build confidence over time.

There are a couple of stereotypes that are very often true that you may or may not have heard that we need to overcome.

Male Stereotype: Men are looking for a "Perfect Ten"

Most men notice physical attributes and raw physical beauty more than women, and certainly tend to fixate on them at times. The Urban Dictionary defines a perfect ten as "A perfect score of 10 out of 10;

as if being scored by judges. Usually pertaining to sexual appeal."[29] This is of course silly as we all have somewhat different tastes and opinions on what constitutes physical beauty.

I'll summarize this with: Men, you want a ten relationship, not merely a woman who is physically a "ten."

Female Stereotype: Women are looking for a man with the right characteristics.

For example, "must love dogs," "doesn't wear socks with sandals," and "has hair," or maybe "doesn't have hair." Women, stop shopping for men with all the right characteristics, you are not shopping for a car or house. You want a man with great character.

And if you are gay or like goats or androgynous space aliens or whatever the same principles apply.

The Big Picture

The big picture is that most successful Infosec Rock Stars also have great personal lives as well.

Yes, they probably have enormous ups and downs like just about everyone else worthwhile. While for some people these ups and downs are merely hills, for some of us they are more like the Himalayas. It doesn't matter; the ups will seem way up and the downs will seem way down, and that's simply a normal part of life.

Positive Influences

The fastest way to become a Rock Star is to hang out with them. Spend time with impressive people. They do not just have to be in Infosec. Read what they write, read what they read, listen to what they say.

---

29   NitsuanNworb. "Perfect 10." *Urban Dictionary*. 17 Nov. 2006. Web. 20 Dec. 2016.

By the way, conferences and local user groups are great ways to connect and meet with others in Infosec and other fields, including some very impressive individuals.

> *You are the average of the five people you spend the most time with."*
> – Jim Rohn

I agree with the sentiment of this statement, although it may not be one hundred percent true. There are always those that rise above their peer group.

I do find inspiration among Rock Stars and aspiring Rock Stars of all types, whether they are serious fly fisherman, winemakers, surfers, marketers, educators, chefs, and more. I find incredible inspiration among Infosec Rock Stars I have the pleasure to hang out with regularly.

Some people are not positive influences. Spend less time with them. In my case these include some old friends who are wonderful people, but their influence on me is definitely not positive. We are still friends, but I simply don't spend a lot of time with them.

Avoiding Burnout – Seven Tips

Burnout typically affects people like us, that is people who are committed to doing a great job and providing significant value. Here are a few tips to help avoid burnout.

1. Take care of yourself.

    We've talked about much of this before, and this includes physical/mental health, good eating habits, getting enough sleep, etc. Of course entire books have been written on various topics of taking care of oneself.

2. Have a hobby; don't be one dimensional!

    Having a hobby apart from anything remotely work related not only makes you a more interesting human, but gives you a break and helps avoid burnout. You use a different skill set than in your work and that is very refreshing.

3. Celebrate victories, both small and large.

    "When you're successful, celebrate, soak it in, and share credit with those who helped you along the way. When other people are successful, celebrate them. Celebrate little successes and big ones. Don't take progress or success for granted. Ever." – Cindy Murphy

4. Manage your time.

    If you don't manage your time, then time will own you. Part of this involves taking time off, whether an hour at lunch, a day, a week, or even fifteen minutes disconnected from your work.

5. Remember, it's just a job.

    "Remember, it's just a job," is tough for most of us, but we cannot take things too seriously. Relax. Even if you are saving the world there will be setbacks.

6. Expect failure.

    The most successful people experience lots of failure. It *is* part of success. Success involves lots of failure along the way. Failures should be learning experiences, or at least interesting data points. More on failure coming up soon.

7. Live today.

*"To live is the rarest thing in the world. Most people exist,
that is all."*
– Oscar Wilde

The best way to avoid burnout is simply to live. Easier said than done, of course.

Living today, not tomorrow because you are too busy, not next week when the project is done, helps avoid burnout.

We all have time crunches when we feel we can barely exist. We may go for days without enough sleep finishing a project. These times will occur, but should be extreme exceptions, not the rule.

Continuing Forward

"It ain't over 'til it's over," said Yogi Berra, a famous American baseball player known for his amusing and sometimes insightful sayings.

I know people in their thirties who think their careers are over. Nothing is going to change; their paths and futures are set.

I also know a man in his early eighties who owns a marina and has plans for massive expansion in the next decade. Who knows if he or the marina will make it, but his attitude is laudable.

There are plenty of people who have gone on to do or continue to do great things in their retirement.

Retirement itself is a quaint idea. It's not like we are longshoremen or do other extremely physical labor and once our bodies age we need to stop. I might be built like a bull moose but I can't keep up with twenty-year-olds physically in the long term. Mentally however, and our work is mental, we can go on for a long time, and experience matters. My father at ninety-four was still pretty sharp and kept up on advances in his field.

Impressive Losers

Here is a list of people with impressive failures and successes. They all achieved significant Rock Star level success. You probably know them all.

Thomas Edison – "Too stupid to learn anything."

Thomas Edison's teachers told him he was "too stupid to learn anything." That was before his over 1000 patents include some earth changing ones. He invented the motion picture camera, the phonograph, and of course the first practical electric light bulb.

Oprah Winfrey – Fired from her first TV job.

Oprah was born into poverty, a victim of sexual abuse during her childhood and early teens, pregnant at fourteen, and fired from her first TV job. She is now a billionaire, was awarded the Presidential Medal of Freedom, and has honorary doctorate degrees from Duke and Harvard.

Dr. Suess – His first book was rejected by twenty-seven publishers.

Theodor Geisel, better known as Dr. Suess, eventually published over 60 books, which were translated into more than 20 languages, with over 600 million copies sold.

Michael Jordan – Cut from his high school basketball team.

Although Jordan didn't make his high school basketball team, he went on to become arguably the greatest basketball player of all time.

Charles Darwin – An average student.

Charles Darwin, an average student, is best known for developing his theory of evolution, which explains biological change. His results were anything but average.

Albert Einstein – Couldn't speak until he was four; did poorly in school; had trouble finding a job.

Einstein is interesting, especially that he couldn't speak until he was four. If a child of mine wasn't speaking until four, I would have had him seen by many specialists.

Walt Disney – Fired from a newspaper because he "lacked imagination and had no good ideas."

Walt Disney lacking imagination is quite amusing.

Rock Star: It's Simple but not Easy

Moving toward Rock Star status is simple, although it's not necessarily easy. There is effort involved and perseverance is needed, as there will be successes *and* failures. Perseverance is not at all hard if you enjoy what you do.

Nothing we have discussed is difficult. It is all simple, but that does not mean trivial. There is more effort involved than just turning on the TV and popping a beer, or grabbing a coffee and a shisha, but it's all simple.

There is work involved. You will need to get out of your comfort zone at times to become a Rock Star, just like a lobster. Why a lobster? Well, lobsters need to regularly shed their hard shells in order to grow. When they shed their hard, protective shell for an initially ultra-soft one, they are truly out of their comfort zone and vulnerable. And although lobsters are regularly extremely vulnerable because of this so called "molting," they can grow to over eighty pounds and live a very long time.

In order to grow, to move towards Infosec Rock Star status, you are going to need get out of your comfort zone sometimes, just like a lobster. You're going to need to look at some new ideas and try some new things and they may not be in your current comfort zone, and that is entirely ok.

You do not need to get far out of your comfort zone like a lobster must when it molts. You can slowly expand your comfort zone while skirting its edges, and don't worry, unlike a lobster, you don't need to worry about getting eaten.

You Should Have a lot of Ideas by Now!

> *"A single thought can revolutionize your life. A single thought can make you rich or well-to-do, or it can land you in prison for the rest of your life.*
> *Everything was an idea before it became real in the world .*
>
> *. .*
>
> *The law of averages begins to swing in your direction when you start to produce ideas. "*
> -Earl Nightingale

Ideas are great and we all have plenty of them. Some will be great, some not so good. Even ordinary people will have extraordinary ideas; we have no shortage. It is taking action on ideas that matters.

Steve Jobs Always Took Action

We are going to (almost) close with the example of Steve Jobs. He wasn't in Infosec and he wasn't even very technical, but he is a great example.

Steve was far from perfect. He smelled bad at times because he didn't bathe often enough. He seemed to suffer enormously from obsessive compulsive disorder. He was extremely harsh on people. He was even unceremoniously dumped with extreme prejudice from Apple, the company he cofounded. His life had massive ups and downs. He made plenty of mistakes. The things he did, the vast majority of them, were simple. They were not necessarily easy but they were all simple. He had extreme passion. It rubbed off on those around them and drove them to extremes to make great stuff. Steve always took action. Often imperfect action, but he took action. Sometimes he obsessed endlessly about things, such as the most minute details of public presentations, but he always took action.

Steve was a true Rock Star. It's your turn; take action!

Take Imperfect Action

"Take Imperfect Action" is a quote from Mario Brown, a guy who arrived in Miami a few years ago nearly broke, speaking poor English, with few prospects. He is doing more than a little well right now; he's married with a new child, living somewhere that appears to be awesome, hanging out with Rock Stars in his field, and has made over $100,000 the first few weeks of this year by providing massive value.

No actions are perfect, and even if they were, how would we know? We need to take action; take imperfect action.

Accountability

Accountability helps us get things done. Good intentions themselves do nothing. It is hard to keep ourselves accountable in the long term if we keep things to ourselves. Even simply writing things down helps a lot. Personally, I like old school pen and paper. Writing things down publically helps more, but may not always be appropriate or desired. Sharing privately with others, especially with one or more who will hold us accountable, can be invaluable.

Action Step: Review the Previous Action Steps from this Book.

I'm sure you have lots of ideas. Write down a list of ideas to move toward Rock Star you may have if you haven't already. You may have different lists for different areas or projects. The previous action steps may help.

Choose one or more ideas and move forward. Consider sharing them with someone else to help keep you accountable.

I could say we end with Action Steps, but as Yogi Berra says, it ain't over until it's over!

For example, I have list of ideas to move forward with the Infosec Rock Star project. I'll be choosing ideas and moving forward, and taking your input to help me decide what to do. This is certainly not the end. There is more coming.

Final Thoughts

Hopefully you've been able to read this with an open mind. Much if this would have seemed very strange to me just a few years ago, yet would have propelled me toward "Rock Star" status much faster.

"Now this is not the end. It is not even the beginning of the end.
But it is, perhaps, the end of the beginning."
– Winston Churchill

"The best way to predict the future is to create it."
– Attributed to Various

I'm busy creating my future, amidst the joy and chaos of ordinary life. Are you creating your future too?

RESOURCES

Be sure to go to http://infosecrockstar.com/bonuses/ and get the extra training videos and resources that go along with this book.

The main Infosec Rock Star website is http://infosecrockstar.com.

Also visit the Infosec Rock Star YouTube Channel.

And find me on twitter at @teddemop.

GLOSSARY

Consultant – A professional who is a subject matter expert in a particular field and provides expert advice. A consultant has a high level of autonomy and will typically consult with several clients within the same time frame, whereas a contractor (below) typically does not.

Contractor – A temporary employee who works closely under a manager's supervision, unlike a consultant. Contractors usually have exactly one client at a time. There absolutely can be some overlap and gray area between "consultant" and "contractor."

Infosec – An abbreviation for "Information Security." As most information today is stored digitally on computers in networks, the terms computer security, IT security, cyber security, and network security are often used nearly synonymously. A closely related term is Information Assurance. Rather than debating the nuances of these terms, we will simply use "Infosec."

Future Orientation – A short statement to help guide your strategic planning, commonly a (Personal) Mission Statement, a *Why*, or a Vision Statement.

Mission Statement – A sentence or paragraph that simply and concisely explains why an organization exists. To make money is rarely the ultimate reason.

Personal Mission Statement – A Mission Statement for an individual. The concept of a Personal Mission Statement originated with Stephen R. Covey in his book, *The 7 Habits of Highly Successful People*.

Punctuated Equilibrium – A theory from evolution that states that usually change is slow to non-existent, a state called stasis. When significant change (rarely) occurs, it tends to be rapid.

Quantum Change – Punctuated Equilibrium on steroids. Massive changes quickly. Often, adapt or die. Rock Stars thrive during Quantum Change. Others may or may not.

Rock Star – Apart from the world of Rock and Roll, a Rock Star is someone who is renowned or revered in their field. Renowned means widely known and revered simply means respected.

Side Gig – Work in addition to your main job or gig. *Gig* is a term originally from jazz musicians in the 1920s, and simply means an engagement, for example to play music or write code. A side gig is typically done to make additional revenue. Your main gig is commonly a fulltime job or contract or consulting in your field of expertise.

Sidepreneur – Someone who has a side gig along with a full time job. An entrepreneur who is building a business on the side along with their regular employment.

Startup – For our purposes we define a startup as a new technology oriented company that has high growth potential and a potentially innovative/disruptive business model.

Statis – A state where change is very slow to non-existent.

Vision Statement – Loosely defined as what you (or an organization) want to become when you grow up. The desired future state.

Why – Your *Why* is a concept from Simon Sinek's TED talk and book called *Start with Why*, which resembles a Personal Mission

Statement. It explains why you do what you do, and can be hard to put accurately into words as it comes from the part of the brain that has no capacity for language.

ABOUT THE AUTHOR

Ted Demopoulos' first significant exposure to computers was in 1977 when he had unlimited access to his high school's PDP-11, and hacked at it incessantly. He consequently almost flunked out but learned he liked playing with computers a lot.

His first professional computer work was in 1984 when he helped work his way through graduate school by programming. In 1986, Ted joined Apollo Computer, where he worked with network administration, security, and user interfaces. He stayed a couple of years beyond the takeover by Hewlett-Packard, and then in 1990, he founded Demopoulos Associates. He has been fortunate since then to be able to work on a number of exciting projects worldwide. Along the way, Ted has also helped start a successful information security company, was the CTO at a textbook failure of a software startup, and has advised several other startups.

Ted is a frequent speaker at conferences, conventions, and other business events, quoted often by the press, and author of several books.

Ted conducts Infosec Rock Star, Leadership, and Information Security classes, and is the principal of Demopoulos Associates, a consulting organization specializing in information security. Ted holds a BA from Dartmouth College and an MS from the University of New Hampshire. More information about Ted is available at www.demop.com.

Ted also managed a couple of rock bands in Boston in the '80s, has seen lots of live music, and likes to experiment with creating interesting food and drink.

Be sure to go to http://infosecrockstar.com/bonuses/ and get the extra training videos and resources that go along with this book.

Morgan James
Speakers Group

www.TheMorganJamesSpeakersGroup.com

We connect Morgan James published authors with live and online events and audiences whom will benefit from their expertise.